# Bright Ideas
# History

## Written and compiled by Lucy Hall

41

Published by Scholastic Publications Ltd,
Marlborough House, Holly Walk,
Leamington Spa, Warwickshire CV32 4LS.

© 1987 Scholastic Publications Ltd

Written and compiled by Lucy Hall
Edited by Jane Hammond
Sub-edited by Melissa Bellamy
Designed by David Cox
Illustrations by Fred Haycock

Printed in Great Britain by
Loxley Brothers Ltd, Sheffield

ISBN 0-590-70804-X

Front and back cover: Martyn Chillmaid, styled by Sally Rowat

# Contents

# Introduction

## Using pictures

Contemporary pictures and paintings provide a vitally important starting point in primary history work. Modern reconstructions and old but non-contemporary illustrations have their uses, but they are not suitable for the very detailed examination that we are considering here.

There are various strategies which encourage children to look closely at pictures and think about what they see, but first discuss with them the partial nature of the evidence. We see only pictures of people who were rich or important enough to have their portraits painted, and few artists painted scenes of ordinary life. If the painter was being paid by the subject of the portrait, what effect was this likely to have had on his work?

## Past and present

Compare features of the picture with things that are within the chidren's own experience. For example:

● Can you think of anyone today who wears a helmet shaped rather like this one? Why were they worn?

● We've found the symbols used by the painter in this portrait of Elizabeth I. What symbols do you think a painter of today might put in a portrait of our present queen? What symbols would you use if you were painting a portrait of your friend or a member of your family?

● Look at the clothes the children in the picture are wearing. Would they be easy to play in? Do you think they are wearing their best clothes or their ordinary clothes? What clothes would you wear if you were having your portrait painted? Would having a portrait painted be more like your mum taking a snap, having a school photograph taken or going to a shop to have your photograph taken by a professional photographer?

## Before and after
Choose a suitable picture (not a portrait) which the children could see as a 'still' – just one in a series of pictures. What happened before and after? There is plenty of material here for discussion, imagination and research. The children could finally paint the series of pictures and display them in a sequence with the original picture.

## A character study
In pictures like Brueghel's which are crammed with characters and action, each child or group can look at one particular character in the picture. What are your characters called?

What sort of people are they? What are their jobs? Where do they live? What are they doing here on this occasion? What were they doing before the time shown in the picture? What will they do afterwards? What might they have said about themselves if they had seen the picture?

## Historical collages
In groups the children could make large collage copies of pictures. The discussion arising from this activity is a vital part of the exercise, so spread your articulate and artistic children evenly among the groups. As they are working in collage, they will have to discuss the precise shape and nature of the objects in the picture. Carefully

chosen pictures should ensure that there are plenty of questions to be answered and facts to be researched.

## On the air
Give each group a different picture and tell them that they are taking part in a television programme called 'The (period you are studying) in Pictures'. Each group must present their picture to a television audience who know little or nothing of the period, explaining the subject matter of the picture and enlarging on what it tells us about the period. You or a child who has been absent and missed the preparation period can be the presenter, introducing each group of experts and their picture to the rest of the class.

## Costume

Costume is one of the easiest and most deluding aspects of historical work in the primary school. It is deluding because carefully copying pictures of 'what they wore' from reference books does not have any educational value or lead to any historical insights. Any study of costume in the past should cast some light on social history and the development of technology.

Today mass production of casual clothing has eroded the traditional function of costume as an indicator of wealth and status. But, when looking at pictures of the past, children can learn quite a lot about what people were like, what position in society they had achieved and what kind of society they lived in simply by studying their clothing.

Clothing changes with the development of trade and technology. From the coarse homespun linen and wool of Saxon times to the silks of the sixteenth century, the massive changes brought about by power spinning and weaving in the eighteenth century, the arrival of cheap cotton which could be washed easily, the discovery of chemical dyes in the nineteenth century, the advent of the sewing machine and, finally, the development of man-made fibres –

MEDIEVAL COSTUME

plain card trimmed with gold braid

chiffon or muslin veil

decoration stuck on

white fur fabric

stiff belt

contrasting coloured underskirt

cardboard spearhead

Balaclava

paper pennant

old jumper

broomstick

shield held on by strip of cardboard

heraldic device painted or sprayed through stencil on to material

tights sprayed silver

all these developments radically affected what people wore.

The people working in the clothing industry are part of the study of costume. Before the eighteenth century richly and elaborately decorated clothes were the product of hours of badly paid, badly lit toil by tailors and seamstresses working by hand. Later, conditions in the mills were even worse. Today, the economy of several developing countries is dependent on the export of cheap clothing to richer countries.

## Handling fabrics

Children's experience of different fabrics may be limited, so a textile table is useful. If you are talking about linen, silk, damask, satin, and so on, the children should be able to handle as many of these fabrics as you can find. Iron the fabrics, cut round the pieces with pinking shears, label them clearly and display them attractively. Ask the children if they can feel the difference between natural materials and synthetics.

Ask a local craft group if anyone can show you examples of some of the crafts which were used when making clothes, such as smocking, embroidery and lace-making.

These fifteenth century head-dresses can be achieved as follows. The sausage shape is made from a tube of brocade or striped fabric, stuffed with rags, cotton wool or crushed tissue-paper. Sew this around a cowl head-dress, and drape over some sheer fabric or decorate with a coloured coxcomb made from felt.

These sixteenth century trousers are made by wearing a pair of baggy trousers over a tighter pair of a contrasting colour. The outer pair is slit and cut off at the knee, then tied with a scarf or wide ribbon.

## What was it like?

Discuss with the children what it must have been like to wear the clothes of various periods. How are they different from clothes today and in other periods, what did they feel like, and how much freedom of movement did they allow? If the clothes weren't easily washed, there was no dry-cleaning and people rarely or never took baths, what did these clothes probably look and smell like? Why did rich people (both men and women) wear a lot of perfume and carry nosegays?

Remind the children that people in portraits were rich people, and talk about the much simpler garments worn by ordinary people.

## Dressing up

For drama, for role-play and for fun, it is difficult to beat dressing up in clothes something like those of the period you are studying. Some museums have replica clothes for children, which are far more realistic than the improvised suggestions shown here, but even the most rudimentary costumes can help children to imagine themselves in the past.

Models can be more accurately dressed; life-sized figures are always popular – draw round a person of the appropriate size lying on the floor and paint the clothes on the figure. Smaller cardboard figures can be dressed more vividly with scraps of material and brightly coloured paper stuck on. Paper clothes with tabs on the shoulders can show the different layers of clothes, although they are fiddly to make.

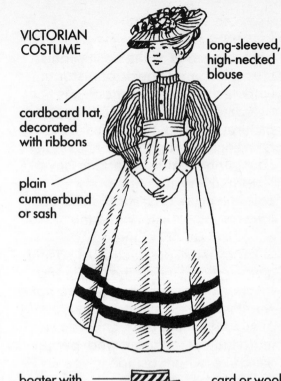

VICTORIAN COSTUME

long-sleeved, high-necked blouse

cardboard hat, decorated with ribbons

plain cummerbund or sash

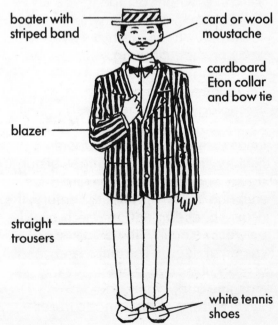

boater with striped band

card or wool moustache

cardboard Eton collar and bow tie

blazer

straight trousers

white tennis shoes

## Services for teachers

Education services vary widely from area to area but, where these services do exist, the take-up by schools is very uneven. Some schools make very full use of all the help that's available, while others never apply at all.

Do remember that education services are just that – services. The people who run them are there to help you and you should not hesitate to find out what they have to offer and how you can use it. Most of the people who run these services are ex-teachers with a sound knowledge of what interests children and a sympathetic understanding of the problems of the non-specialist teacher.

Depending on where your school is situated, you will find at least some of the following services:

### School Library Service

They will send you a collection of books covering the period you are studying which you can keep for a stated period (often a term). Some library services offer multi-media packs and will send you videos, tapes, slides, wallcharts, and so on, as well as books. Through them (or a teachers' centre) you may be able to get recordings of recent schools' broadcasts on your subject, too.

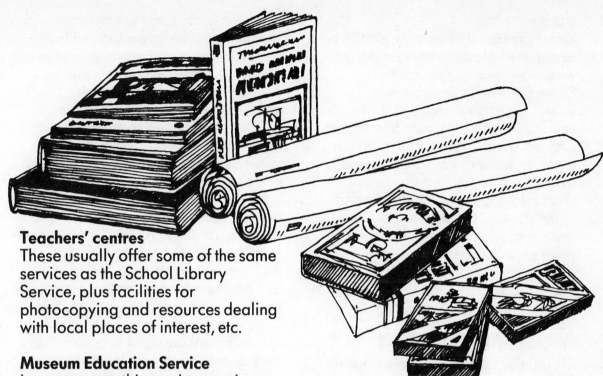

### Teachers' centres

These usually offer some of the same services as the School Library Service, plus facilities for photocopying and resources dealing with local places of interest, etc.

### Museum Education Service

In some areas this service runs in tandem with the School Library Service and in others it is organised separately. (In some areas it doesn't exist!) It is well worth checking to see what your area has to offer; the education officers can be a great help.

A museum may lend items to schools, which provides a valuable opportunity for children to see and handle historical artefacts in the classroom.

Museums with no education service as such may still offer worksheets or other materials for schools and most curators will do their best to help you in any way they can.

Be cautious about very popular exhibits or collections, particularly if you have to travel a long way to get to them. Queuing is not a very educational activity and you should seriously weigh up the value of a day which could cost parents a lot, and which consists largely of travelling and queuing. The children benefit much more from a simpler local excursion with far less expenditure of time and money.

### Local experts

Your librarian will be able to tell you about enthusiasts in various subjects who may live near your school. Someone who is passionately interested in a subject is likely to know a lot about its history, and they may have historical material which they can show to your class. Do talk to enthusiasts yourself first to see what they have to offer which relates to the specific areas you are studying; otherwise you may find yourself a helpless onlooker as your class is swamped with inappropriate and incomprehensible information.

### Individual education services

*Museums and Galleries* and *Historic Houses and Castles*, which should be in your local library, provide detailed lists of museums and historic houses, and the services they offer. The people running these education services will help you to integrate the visit with the rest of your project.

A good education department will offer experiences which become the highlight of any historical project. Particularly popular with children are the places where they can dress up and re-enact activities or events from the past. But these services are booked up months in advance, so you need to do some careful forward planning to take advantage of them.

### The man-made environment

One of the most potent and accessible sources of history for children is provided by the man-made environment – the buildings, street furniture, and so on, which they see all around them.

Norman churches and Tudor mansions are not the only historical sources. There is just as much to learn from the stub ends of iron railings that were taken away in World War II to melt down for armaments, or the bingo hall that used to be a cinema. The kinds of question which children should be encouraged to ask as they look around them are: What exactly is it? Who made it and when? How do we know? Is it still used for the same purpose? If not, why not?

The 'clues for history hounds' on pages 91–93, give very basic information about some major architectural styles of the past. Many buildings or pieces of street furniture are dated or have royal or other monograms to help in dating.

Introduce children to the terms 'pseudo' and 'mock'. How can you tell pseudo-Tudor from the real thing? (The mock beams are too straight and regular, and the building is too square and neat.)

Identify your own local brick style. Nowadays all bricks come from a few large brick-makers, but until about the end of the 1800s, there were thousands of small brickworks all over the country, producing their own distinctive local bricks. The colour of the bricks was determined by the nature of the local clay.

Look at detail and texture in brick and tile patterns, ironwork, chimney pots, fan lights, door knockers, shop fascias and lettering, lamp-posts, letter-boxes, drinking fountains, horse troughs, statues, memorials, gates, archways, and stained and engraved glass.

Taking rubbings helps the children to think about the qualities of various surfaces, and drawing a building carefully and accurately ensures that they really look at it.

Even fairly young children can make judgements about the appropriateness of a building for its function and the aesthetic and practical virtues of various building materials and styles. In most places there will be enough variety of local buildings to offer opportunities for comparisons: eg These flats were built in 1960 and these houses in 1860. Which would you prefer to live in? Why? Were they built for people of similar incomes? What effects have changes in the way people live had on the places where they live? Why were different materials used in 1960? Will they last as long as the materials used in 1860? Why were flats built instead of houses? What sorts of living accommodation are being built in our town today? How do they compare with these buildings?

Your local library, a local preservation society or a keen local architect can pinpoint the buildings and details in your area that are relevant to the period you are studying. If you are taking the children to visit a major historic building, make a preliminary visit first to identify the features that are likely to interest them, to spot viewing places for sketching, to inform yourself as fully as possible about the building and its history, and to plan the work. If you are visiting a building with an education service, make full use of that service, but do plan your own preliminary and follow-up work to lead up to and expand on the work suggested by the service.

## Drama and role-play

Re-enacting events of the past, trying to understand the feelings and motives of people of other times and putting these into words can be a very important and useful part of the historical learning process.

Will it work for your class? The key to successful dramatisation and role-playing is preparation. The children have to understand the issues involved and to be aware of the preoccupations, outlook, fears and beliefs of the people involved. Then they can produce a lively and imaginative dramatisation of an event from the past which will enrich their understanding of it.

Watch out for opportunities for drama and role-play in any history work which has particularly appealed to the children. Perhaps you have been looking at the working conditions of servants in Victorian times, finding out about their wages, hours of work and duties. Suggest that two children might play the parts of the lady of the house and a servant who has come to

be interviewed for a job. Through this role-play, the flesh is put on the bones of the facts, and the relationship between people of different classes at the time is brought vividly to life.

As the culmination of any historical project, a whole-class re-enactment of daily life or events of the time, complete with appropriate names, clothes, food, music and pastimes, provides the children with an unforgettable and rewarding experience, and is well worth the time and effort spent in preparation.

# Throughout the ages

# Dioramas

## Age range
Six to twelve.

## Group size
Three or four.

## What you need
Cardboard cartons, paint, modelling materials.

## What to do
Dioramas – small-scale scenes or models – are particularly useful for historical subjects. They keep a model within reasonable limits (ie the area of a cardboard carton) and provide a built-in backdrop for the scene; they are easily moved about the classroom and written work or background information can be stuck on the outside of the box. They can stand on a table or, with suitable weighting or fixing, on a window sill or narrow surface; alternatively, they can be attached to the wall or hung from the ceiling.

Figure 1

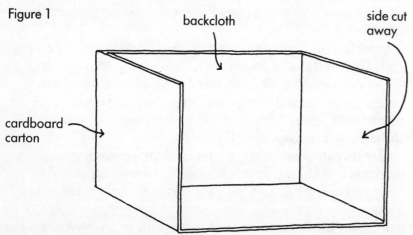

backcloth

side cut away

cardboard carton

Supply boxes of an appropriate size for the subject and the materials you have available. If possible, use white-lined boxes as they provide the best surface for painting.

There is no point in having a top to the diorama unless you need to suspend objects from it or create a cave or cellar, so cut away one of the long sides of the box so that the main backcloth can be painted on the other long side (see figure 1).

The appearance of the diorama is greatly enhanced if the outside of the box is painted or covered. This should be done before the scene inside the box is set up.

Possible subjects for dioramas are:
- Cave paintings: don't cut out the side; just turn the box on its side. Use crumpled black or brown paper to soften the square outlines of the box inside; leave a flat space on the back wall for the paintings, and illuminate it with a 'fire' in the centre of the cave made with real sticks, and a bulb covered in red paper to provide a glow.
- A Viking raid: ships can be painted on the backdrop.
- Building Stonehenge: read Chapter 9 of *Stig of the Dump* by Clive King (Puffin) before starting work on this, and use real stones.

- Roman soldiers on a Roman road: making the road stretch away on the back wall is a good exercise in perspective. At the front edge of the diorama show a section through the road, demonstrating its construction.
- A medieval market-place: remember to include someone in the stocks.
- The battle of the Armada: use Polyfilla or plaster of Paris mixed with blue paint for the sea, and set model ships in it before it is dry so that it holds them fast when it sets.
- The fire of London: use orange and red Cellophane and tissue-paper for flames.
- Scenes from Greek and Roman myths.
- Making a canal or building a railway.
- Guy Fawkes in the cellar of the House of Commons: again, you will need a roof.
- A frost fair on the Thames.
- A blitzed street.
- Armstrong and Aldrin walking on the moon.

# Recreating the past

### Age range
Eight to twelve.

### Group size
Whole class and groups of five or six.

### What you need
Slide projector, camera and film or video-camera and film, material for props and costumes.

### What to do
Do some research to find an event from local history that would be suitable to dramatise. It doesn't have to be a Viking invasion or a Civil War battle – it might be a flood, an influx of evacuees, an industrial dispute or the struggle to create a place to play, or perhaps a famous person lived in the area at some time. Your local librarian should be able to help you. If there are several possible stories, find out which one arouses the most interest among the children.

Start by telling the story of the incident as vividly as you can. Then tell the class that they are going to make a video or slide show of the story. If you have access to a video-camera and someone who can operate it confidently, this is the best medium to use, but a tape-slide show can be very effective.

Divide the class into groups and make each group responsible for a different aspect of the research. Ask them to report back to the class with notes, sketches and ideas.

If possible, arrange a visit to the site or sites where your story occurred, and to any appropriate museums or collections. If the event is within living memory, find eye-witnesses to tell the class about it.

Make sure the children have a good grasp of the story, then make a list together of the various characters involved, rough out the scenes and decide on the shots you will need (about 30 for a slide show).

Give each group a scene to work on and ask them to devise the action and dialogue, including a commentary if they wish. These should be written down and discussed by the whole class before being accepted, rejected or revised for the shooting script.

When the scenes have been polished into their final form, consider sound effects, props, and so on, and cast your characters. Enlist as much help as possible for making props and costumes; aim at bold and simple effects to avoid getting bogged down in detail. Film the crowd scenes first; then most of the children could return to school leaving a small group behind to complete the scenes involving only a few characters. Alternatively, these scenes could be filmed later at school using an unobtrusive background.

If you are using slides, take two or three shots of each scene so that you can select the best one. Putting together the sound-track with narration, dialogue and music will take time and patience; include a signal to indicate slide change.

If possible, edit the video film; save the edited bits — they may prove as popular as the finished story!

Finally, make a display of the props and so on which were involved in the project, and have an official showing of the slide show or video for the rest of the school plus parents.

# Picturing the past

**Age range**
Five to twelve.

**Group size**
Three or four.

**What you need**
Pictures of people or objects from different periods, a large sheet of card, string, wire or rope.

**What to do**
This activity can be used at various levels with children of all ages. Collect a set of about ten pictures of clear, easily recognised stereotypes from different periods, using textbooks, colour supplements, educational magazines, catalogues, advertisements, and so on, as your sources. Choose simple images, such as a dinosaur, a cave dwelling, a Cavalier, a spaceman, a Norman church, a nativity scene, a '30s sportsman or woman, an Edwardian street scene, a World War II servicewoman, an early railway engine, and a pyramid.

Stick your pictures on a sheet of card in random order. Make photocopies of the sheet then try some of the following activities, depending on the age and ability of the children:

● Give each child a copy of the sheet and discuss the chronology of the pictures. Encourage them to use varied and accurate vocabulary to describe people, places and periods. Your set of pictures for this activity could be based on a theme, such as transport.

● Cut up the sheet into separate pictures and laminate or protect each one. Give each child or small group a picture and ask them to write about it – a word, a sentence or a paragraph, depending on their abilities. They could then do some further research into the subject of their picture.

● Run a length of string, wire or rope along the longest wall of the classroom to use as a time-line. Divide a new set of pictures into pairs (one depicting a more recent period than the other).

Give each pair to a group of children and ask them to decide which scene or object is older. Tell them to make up a short statement about it, then get the whole class to vote on which is the oldest in the whole set. Pin that picture to the extreme left-hand end of the line.

Now repeat the process with the second picture in each pair and hold a vote on the most recent image. Place this picture at the right-hand end of the line.

Ask the groups to discuss among themselves where the remaining cards should go (do not worry about how long the gap should be between each picture). Later they can try to place pictures not only in chronological sequence, but also in relative scale. This is easier if you omit pictures of prehistoric subjects so that you are dealing with hundreds rather than millions of years.

As the children become familiar with the process, confine your pictures to a shorter period: eg the earliest picture could show the present queen as a baby, and the latest could show Prince Harry.

## Follow-up

From exercises in sequencing you can go on to the question of authenticity and anachronisms.

Make an odd-one-out card with ten images, one of which is an anachronism. For example, you could have a set of medieval knights, peasants and monks, with a Roman legionnaire amongst them. (Be prepared to accept perfectly logical explanations for the odd-one-out picture which haven't occurred to you.)

Discuss replicas and reproductions. Where do we put a Victorian painting of the nativity on the time-line? What about a replica of Stephenson's rocket, a modern copy of a Greek vase, or the Tudor building down the road which is still doing a roaring trade as a pub?

Children could look through their history books and practise distinguishing between pictures of original artefacts and documents, artists' reconstructions and (more difficult) illustrations which are old but are not contemporary to the period depicted (such as Victorian engravings of sixteenth and seventeenth century events).

Don't forget that 'we don't know', 'it depends' and 'we can only guess' are very valid answers in much history work.

# Inventing history

**Age range**
Eight to eleven.

**Group size**
Whole class and individuals.

**What you need**
Paper for compiling book, material to make book cover, research books.

**What to do**
In most periods of history, you are likely to be finding out about some important invention or discovery of the time. Compiling a class book of inventions will allow everyone to make a contribution on something that interests them. Cover the inventions of your period first, and then you can go forwards and backwards in time.

The account of each invention could include its advantages and disadvantages, and there is plenty of scope for imagination: for example, who invented the wheel? How? What invention of the future would you like to see? The children will also be involved in careful research and factual writing — children who have problems with writing could contribute labelled illustrations (perhaps Heath Robinson style).

# Lighting-up time

**Age range**
Eight to eleven.

**Group size**
Two or three.

**What you need**
Beef or mutton fat (dripping),
cooking oil,
cotton string,
small nails,
screws or washers,
cardboard tubes,
foil,
rubber-bands or sticky tape,
aluminium pie cases,
candles.

**What to do**
Start by talking about what sort of lighting people had in the period you are studying. Few children today come from homes without electricity, so they may find it difficult to grasp that, until gaslights arrived, all lighting was by lamps, lanterns, candles or firelight.

Some children may be familiar with bottled gas lanterns used for camping. It is worth pointing out that lanterns used to have candles inside, and that torches weren't electric but something like tarry rope burning on the end of a stick.

Encourage the children to talk about their experiences of managing without electricity, perhaps during a power cut, than ask them to think about the implications of having only candles or oil lamps all the time. What would the city streets have been like? Is it easy to sew, read or work by candlelight? Would poor people have been able to afford candles? What happened when you went to bed, or if you woke up in the night and wanted to go to the toilet which was outside? How would life be different in winter and summer?

Suggest that they ask the oldest person they know how homes and streets were lit when they were young. They may remember the lamplighter and what he did.

Children will soon begin to realise what life was like after dark up until the nineteenth century, and why it was 'early to bed and early to rise'.

Now go on to make candles and oil lamps. Oil lamps are easy to make. Simply put a little cooking oil in the bottom of an aluminium pie dish, dip in the end of a piece of cotton string for the wick, wind it round the rim and pinch it in place (see figure 1).

For tallow candles, melt the beef or mutton fat over a gentle heat, then pour it into a short section of cardboard

Figure 1

tube with foil taped (or held on by a rubber band) across one end to seal it. Drop a piece of string in the middle weighted at the bottom with a small screw, nail or washer. The children can devise their own methods of holding the wick upright in the middle of the tube until the

fat has set (figure 2). (Supervise the melting of the fat; it should not be hot, just liquid enough to pour.) When the fast has set hard, cut away the cardboard carefully and cut the wick to a suitable length.

Figure 2

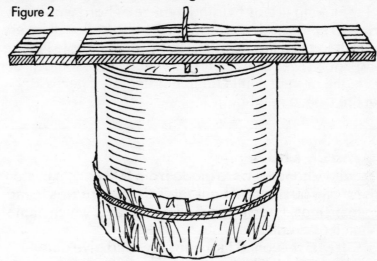

When the children light their lamps and candles (in a blacked-out classroom if possible) they may notice that they are rather smoky and smelly. What effect would this have on people's houses and clothes? You can compare the light of the tallow candles with the light of modern candles which are made of wax.

Discuss how effective a tallow candle is compared with a 100-watt bulb (see fact box on page 20).

How did pre-nineteenth century people light their candles and lamps? Did they have matches? Has anyone heard of a tinder box? What was in it?

## Follow-up
Ask the children to find out about the manufacture of matches, the terrible disease suffered by the girls who worked in the match factories and how they protested about their working conditions. Encourage them to use

19

encyclopaedias and reference books to find out when matches, gaslight and electricity were first used (see fact box), and make a time-line on dark paper with bright symbols marking the significant dates.

Try making fire by twirling a piece of hard wood in a piece of soft wood, as shown in the illustration. It is very difficult to get a flame going, so how did people manage long ago? (They banked fires to keep them going through the night, or kept a little lamp burning or, if necessary, got fire from a neighbour.)

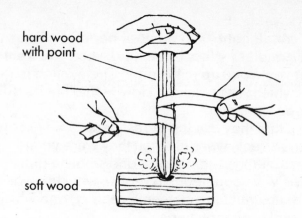

hard wood with point

soft wood

# Fact box

Tallow candles were made from 50 per cent mutton fat and 50 per cent beef fat. This mixture was found to be most effective in making candles which didn't melt or break easily.

It was reckoned that one ox would give about 36kg of suet, which would make 300 tallow candles. A tallow candle needed to be snuffed about eight or ten times an hour (snuffing meant trimming the wick).

Wax candles were about three or four times as effective as tallow candles, smelled less and rarely needed snuffing, but they were much more expensive and only used by the rich – often only for visitors.

A single candle was all the illumination most households used; contemporary illustrations show the woman of the house and her maid servants all sewing by the light of one candle. (A 100-watt bulb is about as effective as 100 wax candles, or about 300 tallow candles!) Rush dips were sometimes used. These were made by stripping the outside off a rush, drying the pith and dipping it in fat.

A tinder box contained a flint and a piece of fire steel with the tinder, which was usually charred rag or sometimes dried tree fungus. The steel and flint were struck together to make a spark with which the tinder was kindled. This was not an easy task: there were very few housemen or maids who could strike a light in less than three minutes.

The friction match was invented in 1826 and the safety match in 1855.

Paraffin was used from about 1830. The Royal Pavilion in Brighton was lit with gas in 1818 and the first gas street lamps appeared in Pall Mall in 1907. Gas lighting, once again, was used in homes only by the more prosperous, and one of the attractions of the 'gin palaces' was that they were brilliantly lit by gas, in contrast to the barely lit homes of the poor.

The first electric street lights were used in Holborn Viaduct in 1882, and the first domestic electric lights were used in about 1880, but it was a long time before the majority of homes had electric lights.

Gas was used for street lighting well into this century, and even people in their fifties can remember the lamplighters who had long poles with a light at the end which were poked up into street lamps to turn on the gas and light them.

# Hill figures

**Age range**
Eight to twelve.

**Group size**
Whole class.

## What you need
Pictures of hill figures, library books on hill figures (*Gods and Graven Images: the Chalk Hill Figures of Britain* by Paul Newman (Robert Hale) is useful), 5cm squared paper, chalk, string and pegs, sports ground line-marking machine (if working on grass).

## What to do
Find out if any of the children have seen a hill figure, and ask them what it depicted. (Dorset teachers who are not prepared for intimate discussions about the Cerne Giant's anatomy might do well to avoid this topic!)

If no-one has seen a hill figure, you will have to start your discussion with the pictures.

Who made the figures and how? What sort of hillside is needed for a figure? (Grass on chalk.) Will the figure be permanent? (Only if the turf is kept cut back from the exposed chalk.)

Explain that we know very little about who cut most of the figures or why. The obvious exceptions are the modern figures: for example, the Whipsnade lion, and the regimental crests on the hillside at Fovant in Wiltshire, which were cut in World War I by troops stationed in the area.

There are many theories about older figures, such as the Long Man of Wilmington. Some say that the Long Man was a landmark for pilgrims to direct them to the priory below; others that it was the 'fighting man' – a device used by Harold the Saxon – and that it therefore dates back to Saxon times. Still others believe that it was a Roman emperor cut by Roman soldiers, while some say it is a Hindu or Scandinavian god (Varuna or Odin), and others that it is an eighteenth century gentleman's folly.

Find out what the children think. Explain that 'experts' have come up with all sorts of theories and dates for the Long Man – and these accounts are highly contradictory. All we really know is that the first recorded mention of the figure was made in the eighteenth century, so it is at least as old as that.

Ask the children to look carefully at the figure and then write their own story about who made the Long Man, when and why. Some of them might like to try writing their story as a ballad. They could use white chalk, paint or pastel to draw the Long Man to scale on green paper (see figure 1). Mount the stories and poems on green paper and display them round the figure with the headline 'Our solutions to the mystery of the Long Man of Wilmington'.

Now you can make your own hill figure. Discuss what it might depict – perhaps the school crest, a local coat of arms, a school pet, the hero of a favourite story, a local sporting figure, or an imaginary character. Each child can then draw in bold felt-tipped pen an outline of the figure he or she has chosen; remind them to keep it simple.

Exhibit all the pictures and vote on which one you will use. The originator can then transfer the design to 5cm squared paper.

Measure the area available and work out how big the figure can be. It has to be transferred from the 5cm squared grid to a large grid on the ground. What scale will be needed for the large grid?

Mark out the grid in coloured chalk on the playground or with string and pegs on the field, then show the children how the lines on the 5cm squares can be transferred fairly accurately to the larger squares on the ground.

Everyone should have a turn at marking part of the outline. Use white chalk on the playground, and paint it over with white emulsion paint later if you can get permission for a more permanent figure. Use a line-marker on the field if you can get hold of one; otherwise use strips of white cloth pegged to the grass.

The children will learn the difficulties of working close up to a large figure designed to be seen from a distance.

When your figure is complete, try to find a high vantage point from which to view it – bear this in mind when you first choose the site.

Figure 1

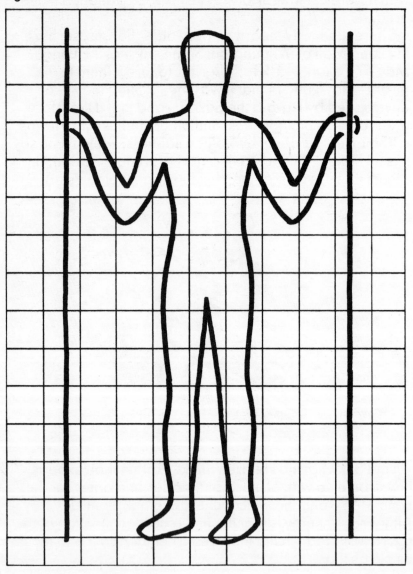

# Fact box

## Hill figures (with dates)

White Horse of Uffington, Oxfordshire – Celtic or
    Saxon.
Long Man of Wilmington, Sussex – Celtic or Saxon.
Cerne Giant, Dorset – Celtic or Romano-British.
Bledlow Cross, Buckinghamshire – medieval.
Whiteleaf Cross, Buckinghamshire – seventeenth
    century.
Watlington White Mark, Buckinghamshire –
    1764.
New Westbury Horse, Wiltshire – 1778.
Cherhill Horse, Wiltshire – 1780.
Osmington White Horse, Dorset – c1800.
Marlborough Horse, Wiltshire – 1804.
Alston Barnes Horse, Wiltshire – 1812.
Woodbury Horse, Hampshire – c1840.
Kilburn White Horse, Yorkshire – 1857.
Broad Town Horse, Wiltshire – 1864.
White Stag of Strichen, Aberdeenshire – 1870.
White Horse of Strichen, Aberdeenshire – 1900.
Wye Crown, Kent – 1902.
Bulford Kiwi, Wiltshire – 1914–1918.
Fovant Regimental Badges, Wiltshire – 1916–1918.
Buffs Badge, Canterbury, Kent – 1922.
Litlington Horse, Sussex – 1925.
Hackpen Horse, Broad Hinton, Wiltshire – 1935.
Whipsnade Lion, Bedfordshire – 1935.
Pewsney New Horse, Wiltshire – 1937.
Laverstock Panda, Wiltshire – 1969.

There are other hill figures, ancient and
comparatively modern, which are known to have

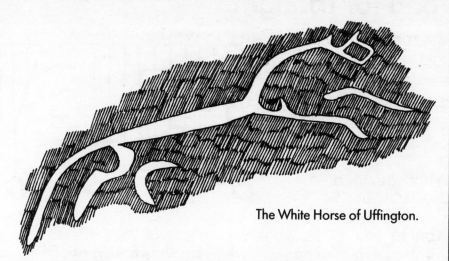

The White Horse of Uffington.

existed but which have become overgrown and
disappeared. Maintaining a chalk figure is quite a
task and, over the years, changes can occur. The feet
of the Long Man are believed to have been altered
when it was restored in 1874, and at one time his two
staves were a scythe and a rake.

The scouring of a hill figure used to be an annual
event in some places (often at Whitsun or
Michaelmas) accompanied by a 'pastime' or fair.
Today figures are looked after by local preservation
societies, the Department of the Environment or the
National Trust.

The Bulford Kiwi used to be maintained by the Kiwi
polish company and when the company withdrew in
1967, the figure became very overgrown and almost
disappeared. It was restored in 1981 by the 249
Signals Squadron, NATO; 160 officers and men
worked 12 hours a day for three days to clear the
vegetation and dig the outline to a depth of 30cm.
The Kiwi is 128m long with a 46m beak.

23

# Food for thought

**Age range**
Eight to twelve.

**Group size**
Whole class and pairs.

**What you need**
Copies of page 94.

## What to do

Distribute copies of page 94, which shows two ways of turning the spit on which meat was roasted in front of an open fire, until the introduction of the kitchen range in 1780. The whole animal or joints of it were impaled on a bar which rested on the stand. It had to be turned so that the meat cooked evenly. In large households this was sometimes done by a small boy holding up a wet blanket or an old straw arrow target to protect himself from the heat, and sometimes by a dog working a treadmill.

Page 94 is intended to spark off discussion about food and cooking in the past. It is difficult for children accustomed to the range and variety of foods today to realise how very limited their ancestors' diets were, and how simple their cooking methods. What would it be like living in a house with no windows or chimney where the cooking in winter was done on an open fire? What sorts of things did people eat in the period you are studying?

Ask the children to imagine that they are going round the supermarket and choosing food. Draw three large trolleys on the board, labelled 'yes', 'no' and 'don't know'. As the children think of a food, they must decide which trolley to put it in according to whether it was available in the period you are studying. This will give rise to many questions and much discussion. If you find that the 'don't know' list is getting too long, you may have to provide some guidance (see fact box) but, as far as possible, let the children work it out for themselves or do research to find out once they have completed the lists.

Your 'yes' trolley will probably need a division to separate the foods that were only available to the more prosperous, and it is worth reminding the children that the supermarket itself is an anachronism. Most people, particularly before the Industrial Revolution, had to be self-sufficient, producing their own food rather than buying it from shops.

Were people able to preserve foods in this period? The techniques of drying, smoking and salting are very old and children can try to identify which foods belong in these categories. Ordinary people could not obtain or afford imported foods until the nineteenth century, although spices (most useful for disguising the taste of rotten meat), oranges, figs, dates, nuts, and so on, were available to the rich from Tudor times.

The diet of poorer people in winter was very limited indeed – bread, root vegetables, salt pork, cheese and perhaps a bird or rabbit. By the end of the winter they would be thin and weak. It was not only sailors who got scurvy. In the spring a kind of grass known as scurvy grass was eagerly searched out and eaten together with the early green shoots on the hawthorn.

When the children have done their research and the foods are all sorted out into the 'yes' and 'no' trolleys, ask them to devise and illustrate some menus for your period – first the food they would eat in a day if they were poor, in summer and in winter, and then a feast for their friends if they were rich. Display the menus around two large cut-outs of the trolleys, containing the lists of foods.

# Fact box

Prehistoric people would have eaten deer, hares, birds, birds' eggs, fish, shellfish, berries, fruits, nuts, mushrooms, leaves, some kinds of root, and honey.

During the New Stone Age, people learned to farm. They grew grain and kept tamed farm animals.

Grains (wheat, oats, barley and rye) could be ground to a rough flour between stones and then baked as bread in the ashes of the fire or boiled to a sort of porridge. Grains could also be fermented to make ale. Cattle, sheep, pigs and goats were kept for meat and milk, as well as leather and horn to make drinking cups, skins for clothing and wool. Fowls, ducks and geese were kept for meat, eggs and feathers, and bees for honey.

Until two or three hundred years ago, farmers could not feed many animals through the winter. When the grass stopped growing at the start of winter, most of the meat animals had to be killed and the meat preserved by salting (salt was a vital commodity – hence the superstition that it is unlucky to spill salt), smoking and drying, or combinations of these processes.

The Romans are said to have introduced pheasants and rabbits, and they improved wine production. In the 1500s French beans, lettuce, rhubarb and carrots were introduced.

In the 1600s food from the newly discovered Americas began to arrive – turkeys and potatoes. New drinks appeared during this period too – chocolate from Central America, coffee from Arabia and tea from China. These imports were all very expensive and were either drunk at special shops or, in the homes of the rich, were kept under lock and key. The price of tea fell when it began to come from India as well as China, but most tea-leaves were still brewed three times – first for a well-to-do family, then for their servants, and then the twice-used leaves were dried and passed on to the servants' families and friends.

Sugar had been available since the Crusades but only as a very rare luxury (honey was used as a sweetener). It wasn't until the 1800s that sugar and imported drinks were generally used. However, during the seventeenth century, housewives increasingly used sugar to preserve fruit as jam and for making crystallised fruits and flowers.

Tinned foods came on the market in the late 1800s. Tomatoes had been around for a long time, but they were believed to be poisonous and weren't eaten until the end of the 1800s. Breakfast cereals were introduced in the early 1900s. Frozen foods were first sold in this country in 1937 but they did not become commonly used until the 1950s.

# Quill pens

### Age range
Nine to twelve. Younger children can try using quill pens, but you may not want them to use the tools involved in making them.

### Group size
Individuals.

### What you need
Preferably goose quills (but you can try turkey quills or other strong feathers), craft knives or Stanley knives.

### What to do
Shorten the quill to about 20cm by cutting off the top, then strip all the barbs from the shaft, pulling downwards. Cut the end off the bottom of the shaft with a sharp craft or Stanley knife. (See figure 1.)

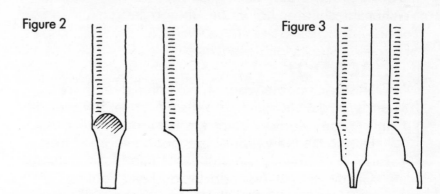

Figure 1

Cut away the bottom of the quill (see figure 2) for about 15–18mm, and remove its core with fine tweezers. Make a slit in the end of the nib about 5mm long, then pare the sides of the point to make a nib shape (see figure 3).

Figure 2                                    Figure 3

Finally, cut off the extreme tip of the nib at an angle, resting the nib on the edge of the cutting board (see figure 4).

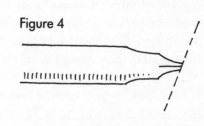

Figure 4

Although the children will be using craft knives, they will soon understand how the pen-knife got its name and why many people carried them. They may have seen quills used in historical dramas which have all the barbs still on them, but you can assure them that this is incorrect.

The children can use the pens to try elaborate signatures like that of Elizabeth I (see illustration), or for writing 'historical' documents (see pages 67 and 70).

### Follow-up
Try using other writing implements – brushes, reeds, bamboo, and so on – particularly for Chinese calligraphy.

# Your parish church

**Age range**
Six to twelve.

**Group size**
Whole class.

## What you need
Permission to visit the church, other adults to help, copies of page 95, clip boards, pencils etc.

## What to do
Make a preliminary visit to the church yourself so that you can find potentially interesting features. Talk to the vicar about these features and find out when is a suitable time for a visit. If the church has a tower and/or bells, arrange to go up the tower and into the belfry if possible.

Unless the vicar is an exceptionally fascinating talker, explain tactfully that you want the children to find things out for themselves and ask him to be there just to answer questions briefly. Gather any leaflets or other written material about the church and ask about the boundaries of the parish.

In the classroom, start by asking the children if they know what parish the school is in (see fact box on page 29). Do they know where the parish church is, what it is called and who worships there? Explain that you are going to visit the church and, using local maps, make a map of your parish showing the school and the church. Then work out the best route to the church. (Obviously some of these activities are inappropriate for church or village schools where the school is close to the church and the children are familiar with it.)

You could either give each child a worksheet with prepared questions, or give different groups of children specific things to investigate. Alternatively you could wait to see what captures their interest and follow up on this.

27

Before you go, draw a plan of the church, label the main features — the font, lectern, altar, pulpit, vestry, tower, organ, and so on — and talk about their functions so that the children will have some basic knowledge to start with. Also discuss the kind of behaviour that is appropriate to a place of worship, and if there are any places they mustn't enter. As you approach the church ask the children to stop and look at the whole building and its surroundings. This will help them to find their bearings once they are inside.

Tell them to look for the following features:

Parish notices in the porch.

A list of previous rectors — if this goes back far enough you may notice periods when the rector was only in charge for a short time; this could be due to pestilence or religious change.

Windows — if there is any stained glass, when does it date from and what does it show? Make sketches to be worked on later in the classroom.

Brass and stonework — make rubbings if you have permission.

Memorial plaques — copy the wording on any interesting plaques; they often reveal a lot about the history of the area.

Symbols — the symbols of the saint to whom the church is dedicated may be displayed in different ways; look, too, to see how often the cross recurs.

Organ — where and when was it made, and how does it work? (Arrange for a demonstration, if possible.)

War memorials and battle colours — to which war do these refer, and what local regiments are associated with the church?

Bells — where and when were they cast, do they have names, who rings them, when are they rung, when were they rung in the past, and what was the longest peal ever rung?

Architecture — which features of the building help to tell us when the church was built (see pages 91–93), is the whole building of the same age, and if not, when were different parts built?

Registers — what are the parish registers for, how far do they go back, is the christening of someone in the class or the wedding of someone's parents recorded in one of the registers, and can you see some of the oldest registers? In old registers you may be able to see places where people have signed with a cross because they couldn't write.

Refuge — has the church ever acted as a refuge in times of disaster or emergency?

Special features – look for carved pew ends, gargoyles, sundials, carved figures on tombs, and so on.

In the churchyard remind the children, once again, about appropriate behaviour before they look round the graveyard. The children could try to find the earliest date on the gravestones, although some of the very old ones will be difficult to decipher. (Have copies of page 95 on Roman numerals with you.)

They may notice the large number of children whose names appear on the older gravestones – a vivid reminder of the health hazards and very high child mortality rates of earlier times. If there is a whole crop of dates occurring at about the same time, you could try to find out why. Was there an epidemic of some kind?

Make rubbings of any particularly interesting inscriptions. (The rector can tell you about these beforehand, so that you can point them out if no-one finds them.)

Is there a yew tree by the church gate? This is fairly common. Why? Finally sit everyone down to make drawings of the church from any angle they choose.

## Follow-up

Paint stained glass windows from the sketches made at the church. Oil the back of the paper to make it transluscent, cut out the paintings and stick them to the classroom windows.

Write any interesting epitaphs or memorials in a booklet cut out in the shape of a tombstone.

Finish off the pencil sketches of the church in ink, mount and display them round a plan view of the church with arrows to show where each drawing was made.

Visit other places of worship, such as a mosque, a synagogue, a Hindu temple and a gurdwara, and encourage children from those faiths to discuss their customs, beliefs, and the history behind them.

## Fact box

Some English parishes date from the late 600s, and the whole country was divided into parishes by the mid-1300s. As towns grew, parishes had to be divided to serve the growing population, particularly in the 1800s. A church in a later style of architecture may belong to one of these new parishes, or it may have been built to replace an old church that was destroyed or crumbled away.

Each parish belongs to a diocese under a particular bishop. Again, the country was divided into dioceses in the thirteenth century, and these were subdivided as the population grew. Most of the new dioceses were made in the 1900s.

The rector in each parish was paid by tithes by law from 1285 (one tenth of the crops his parishioners grew and the animals they raised) until 1836 when a rent charge was substituted. In some places a tithe barn – used to store the tithes – still survives.

# The ancient world

# Modern mummies

**Period**
Ancient Egypt.

**Age range**
Five to ten.

**Group size**
Two or three.

**What you need**
Small life-like dolls,
sequins, card,
shoe-boxes,
cling-film,
plaster of Paris
or Polyfilla,
old bandages
or strips of white
cotton material,
paint,
varnish (optional),
PVC glue.

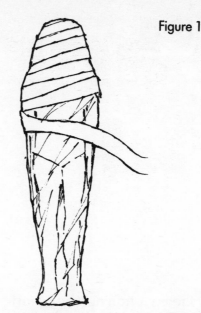

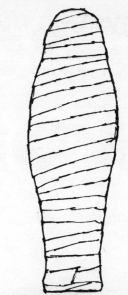

Figure 1

Figure 2

## What to do
The children must imagine that the dolls are Ancient Egyptians who have just died. Who are they? How did they die? When a suitable biography has been created for each doll, the mummification can begin.

Cover the dolls completely with food-wrapping film first to protect them. Then bind them tightly with old bandages or strips of white cotton material, until a satisfactory mummy shape is achieved. Glue the end of the bandages of cloth in place with PVC glue. (See figure 1.)

Mix plaster of Paris or Polyfilla to a stiff consistency and spread it all over the bandages. This is very messy so do it outside if possible.

While the mummies dry, the children can paint and decorate the shoe-boxes. Then the mummies can be painted and perhaps varnished. When they are completely dry, put them in the shoe-box sarcophagi (see figure 2).

Display the mummies with written work or drawings on scrolls alongside them, giving their biographies or an account of the (real) mummification process.

# Egyptian numbers

**Period**
Ancient Egypt.

**Age range**
Eight to twelve.

**Group size**
Whole class and pairs.

**What you need**
Copies of page 96.

**What to do**
Give each child a copy of the Egyptian number chart (page 96), then write an Egyptian number on the board (see illustration) and ask them what number it is. Explain that Egyptian numbers were written from right to left and that the number shown is 23. Once the children understand this, write up some number sentences at an appropriate level for them to complete. Then they can devise calculations for their friends to do.

**Follow-up**
Make up an Egyptian quiz with questions requiring numerical answers, which must be given in Egyptian numerals (eg How many vertices has a pyramid?)

# Egyptian measurement

**Period**
Ancient Egypt.

**Age range**
Eight to twelve.

**Group size**
Whole class and pairs.

**What you need**
Copies of page 97.

**What to do**
Explain that the Egyptians used body units of measurement – digits, palms and cubits (see page 97). What are the advantages and disadvantages of using body units of measurement?

Then, working in pairs, they can make a table of the metric equivalents of digits, palms and cubits, based on their own body measurements. Do seven of their palms equal one of their cubits?

You could establish the class extremes and average for each measurement, or find out if the tallest people always have the longest cubit measurement.

**Follow-up**
The children may remember the story of the building of Noah's ark (*Genesis* 6 vv 14–16). Using an agreed standard cubit, the children could measure the dimensions of an ark on the playground and draw a plan and elevation in chalk.

Then they can use calculators to work out the size of the ark measured in their own cubits, and make scale drawings of it on squared paper.

# Going Greek 1 – Pendants

**Period**
Ancient Greece.

**Age range**
Eight to eleven.

**Group size**
Individuals.

**What you need**
Papier mâché, self-hardening clay
or thick card and silver foil,
copies of page 98,
chain, leather thong, cord or thick string.

**What to do**
Get the children to study the alphabet sheet to see the Greek version of their initial or any letter they choose. Then ask them to make pendants of that shape using papier mâché, self-hardening clay or thick card covered with silver foil.

Pierce the letter shape (before it hardens if you are using papier mâché or clay) and thread it on a chain, leather thong, cord or thick string.

# Going Greek 2 – Columns

**Period**
Ancient Greece.

**Age range**
Eight to eleven.

**Group size**
Individuals, twos or threes.

**What you need**
White cartridge paper,
cheese boxes,
shallow rectangular
boxes or box lids,
white paint,
sticky tape.

**What to do**
Models of Greek buildings are easily constructed from cardboard boxes. To make Doric columns, start with rectangles of cartridge paper, pleat them and then shape the pleated paper into a cylinder. Secure the cylinder with sticky tape, and place a cheese box and rectangular box on top. Paint the column white.

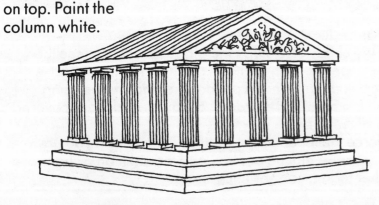

# Going Greek 3 – Coins

**Period**
Ancient Greece.

**Age range**
Nine to eleven.

**Group size**
Individuals.

**What you need**
Card, PVC glue,
string,
aluminium foil,
soap (optional),
black paint (optional).

Figure 1

**What to do**
Before beginning to make their coins, the children can study pictures of Greek coins to give them ideas for designs. They could copy the head of Athene on one side, and her bird (the owl) with a branch from her sacred olive tree on the other (see figure 1).

They should begin by cutting out a card disc then building up a design by sticking other pieces of card on to it – first a basic head-shape in profile, then locks of hair, an eye, a headband, and so on. Glue a circle of string round the edge of the disc as a border. (See figure 2.)

Figure 2

When the glue is dry, cover the disc with foil, smoothing it down carefully so that the design shows through. Ease it round the edges and secure it with glue or sticky tape on the back of the disc. If the children are building designs on both sides, cover each side with foil, then trim and smooth the edges.

If the children want the coins to look old and worn, prepare the foil beforehand by screwing it up tightly to crinkle it, then opening it out carefully and smoothing it out. Rub a paintbrush on the soap and paint the foil with black paint, repeating the soaping frequently to help the paint stick to the foil. When it is dry, rub the foil briskly with a piece of rough cloth or crumpled paper towel, being careful not to tear the foil. Most of the paint will come off, but enough will be left in the cracks to give an antique effect.

# Going Greek 4 – Stencils

## Period
Ancient Greece.

## Age range
Nine to eleven.

## Group size
Individuals.

## What you need
Card or strong brown paper, stiff brushes, brown, black and white paint, small scissors with points.

## What to do
Get the children to make simple repeating designs based on the border patterns on Greek pottery, then draw them on card or brown paper and cut them out carefully to make stencils.

They can then use these stencils on vases (see page 37), book covers, and so on. Tell them to hold the paintbrush upright and brush from the edges towards the middle of the stencil to avoid smudging. (Use the brown paper stencils shiny side up.)

# Going Greek 5 – Masks

### Period
Ancient Greece.

### Age range
Nine to eleven.

### Group size
Individuals.

### What you need
Thin strong card, paper, glue.

### What to do
The stylised masks used in the Greek theatre are interesting to copy.

   To make a mask, the children should cut out oval shapes from strong card and cut openings for the eyes and mouth. How will these differ for tragic and comic masks?

Then show them how to cut and fold noses from card (see figure 1) and make paper coils or spirals for hair. Cut slots in the mask to fit the tabs on the nose (see figure 2), push the tabs through the slots and glue them in position at the back of the mask. Then glue on the hair.

Figure 2          Figure 1

Each child can paint or decorate his mask, then staple it to a strip of card, about 4cm wide, which has been stapled in a circle to fit his head.

# Going Greek 6 – Vases

## Period
Ancient Greece.

## Age range
Eight to eleven.

## Group size
Individuals or pairs.

## What you need
Glass jars or bottles,
petroleum jelly,
wallpaper paste,
newspaper,
white drawing paper
or newsprint,
brown, black and white paint,
pictures or reproductions
of Greek pottery.

## What to do
Cover the lower straight-sided part of a jar or bottle with petroleum jelly. Then stick on overlapping squares of white paper until the greased area is covered (figure 1).

Figure 1

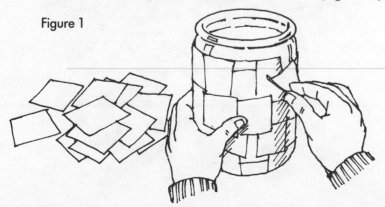

Now repeat the process with squares of newspaper, leaving no white gaps. Continue pasting on alternate layers of white paper and newspaper until you have built up about seven layers, finishing with a white layer.

Put the jar in a warm place until the paste is completely dry, then ease it out of the paper case. Now the case can be decorated by painting or printing on it with brown, black and white paint.

The children should have a chance to study pictures of Greek pottery first, or see the real thing in a museum. Somebody might be able to lend the reproduction plates or vases that are made in Greece for the tourist trade. All these will give the children ideas for colours, patterns and figures. (See also page 35.)

You could also paint disposable paper plates with Greek designs and figures.

# Popular myths

## Period
Ancient Greece and Rome.

## Age range
Six to twelve.

## Group size
Any size.

## What you need
The widest possible range of materials.

## What to do
When the children have heard or read a selection of myths, let them choose their favourite stories to act, mime and illustrate. These myths have a powerful hold on children's imaginations and you can encourage them to use all sorts of media to reflect their responses.
● They could make their own music or choose a favourite record to accompany mime.

● Try newspaper reports ('ODYSSEUS HOME AT LAST – SUITORS SLAIN').
● Make highly illustrated maps to show different events and where they occurred, and to plot voyages. You could base these on modern maps of Greece.
● Cut out people-sized models of the gods, paint them and hang them from the classroom ceiling. Atlas could be made big enough to reach from floor to ceiling and placed in a corner of the classroom, 'supporting' the ceiling on his shoulders.
● After miming Theseus' journey through the labyrinth and his battle with the Minotaur, make a huge labyrinth for the classroom wall, with the battle raging at the centre and a coloured string marking the way through the labyrinth.
● Model Medusa's head in clay or display the story of the Gorgons on a cut-out of her head with spiral paper snakes for hair.
● Divide the class into 12 groups, give each group a very large sheet of paper and ask each of them to illustrate

one of the Labours of Hercules in whatever medium they choose. Mount and title all the pictures in the same style, and display them side by side down a corridor.

• Use collage for the story of Odysseus and his six companions escaping from the Cyclops. The sheep could be made from crumpled tissue-paper or scraps of carpet, and Cyclops' blinded eye from red shiny paper.

• Get the children to make up the song of the sirens, record it and play it while they mime the ship passing the island – Odysseus, lashed to the mast, writhes to get free, and his crew, with their ears blocked, carry on sailing the ship.

• Divide the class into Greeks and Romans and act the building of the wooden horse and the discussion amongst the Trojans before they haul it into Troy (with the Greeks sitting inside and being thrown about). Then, while the Trojans sleep, the Greeks stealthily descend to let their comrades into Troy. Make a class frieze to show the Trojans hauling the horse into Troy, with a flap on the side of the horse which lifts to show the Greeks inside.

• Display poetry about Jason and the golden fleece on a 'fleece' made from gold paper strips which have been curled round a pencil. Use more gold paper for the cover of a book containing retellings of the Midas story.

• Make steep slopes with forms hooked on to wall bars in the gym or hall, to mime the torture of Sisyphus forever rolling his stone uphill only to have it roll down again. Choose the best mime for everyone to watch before they make their own models from clay, perhaps incorporating a real stone instead of a clay one.

• Suggest strip cartoons or zigzag books to tell the story of the Odyssey or the voyage of the Argonauts.

• Each child could decorate a paper or pottery plate with a scene from a different myth (see pages 35 and 37).

Make this the opportunity for the children to think of all the various media and techniques they have ever used and to select the one they feel best suits the myth they have chosen.

# Roman to medieval

# How long is a mile?

## Period
Romans to Middle Ages.

## Age range
Nine to twelve.

## Group size
Individuals.

## What you need
Copies of page 99, calculators.

## What to do
Write the question 'How long is a mile?' on the board and put the children's answers underneath. They may need reference books to help them, but they are likely to decide that a mile is 1760 yards or 1602 metres or 1.6 kilometres (or eight furlongs). Make sure you get the answer in yards. Now distribute copies of page 99 and suggest that the initial question needs some amendment: for instance, 'How long is a modern mile?' or 'How long has a mile been since 1588?'

When the children have agreed on an alternative question, ask them to answer the quiz questions on the sheet. Then they can choose an old mile from the list and make up their own quiz for their friends, displaying their chosen mile's length on a drawing of a milestone at the top of their quiz.

It will save time and argument to phrase the questions in the following form: 'If it is x modern miles from y to z, how far is it in (their choice of) miles?' Alternatively, they could start with the distance in old miles and ask for an answer in modern miles.

This gives plenty of conversion practice as they convert modern miles to yards and yards to old miles, and vice versa.

You may find it best to work with a group of slower children on the easier questions in the quiz and help them to make up and answer some questions themselves, while the other children work at their own pace on the quiz questions and then their own quizzes.

## Fact box
The Latin word for a thousand is 'mille', so the distance a Roman soldier could cover in a thousand paces became known as a mile. The Romans put milestones along their roads in Britain, some of which can still be seen today.

A Roman pace was in fact two strides, and the Roman mile was about 1,618 yards long.

For a long time after the Romans, there were all sorts of different miles. It wasn't until 1588, in Elizabethan times, that the length of the mile was fixed at 1,760 yards – the length it is today. The length of a yard was fixed much earlier and so, by converting to yards, we can compare these old miles to ours.

# Reporting on the Romans

**Period**
Romans.

**Age range**
Eight to twelve.

**Group size**
Any size.

**What you need**
Magazines,
colour supplements etc,
large sheets of paper.

**What to do**
When the children have done some work on various aspects of Roman life, suggest that they present what they know about the Romans in the form of a magazine or newspaper. Discuss the kinds of feature that might be included (fashion, cooking, sport, news, health, letters, home-making, agony column, advertisements etc).

As a suggestion for agony column letters, point out that a Roman soldier would not regard a posting to Britain with much enthusiasm, rather like a British soldier having to go to the Falklands today. What would they miss? What would their impressions of Britain be?

The children may need to carry out further research to find the details they need.

The magazine covers could be done in mosaic style using bits of coloured paper cut or torn from magazines, colour supplements, and so on.

This is a lively and enjoyable way of summarising and reflecting work done on any period – not just the Romans. It gives a purpose to research and allows plenty of opportunities for children to use their imaginations in trying to empathise with people of a different time. It can also produce some very imaginative and amusing results.

# Roman plaques

## Period
Romans.

## Age range
Eight to twelve.

## Group size
Individuals.

## What you need
Clay, clay tools, plaster, cheese boxes, nails or pairs of compasses, paint or shoe polish, pictures of Roman bas relief (carvings in stone) in reference books, pieces of card.

## What to do
Tell the children that much of what we know about Roman life has been learned from their carvings in stone which have lasted through the years. (Introduce the term 'bas relief' to older children.) Ask them to find pictures of stone carvings in the reference books on the Romans.

When they have studied some of these pictures, ask them to choose some aspect of Roman life which they have found interesting to represent in clay or plaster bas relief. Suggest that they make a rough drawing first.

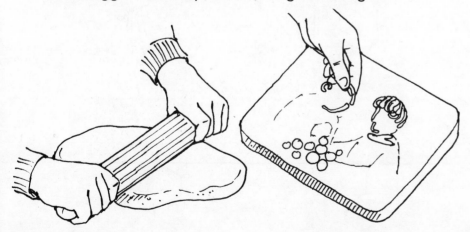

Clay should be rolled out to a thickness of about 3cm; this can then be cut to various shapes. Leave it to dry out for a little while before starting work. The children can build up their scenes with small clay shapes and coils, as well as by scratching into the surface of the clay.

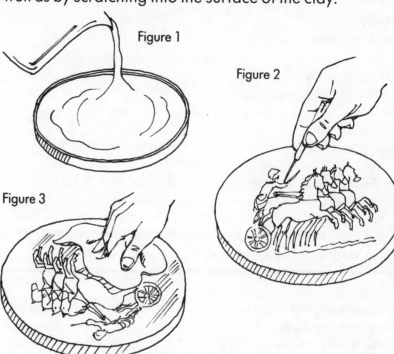

Figure 1

Figure 2

Figure 3

For plaster plaques, use two parts plaster to one part water, pour the mixture into a cheese box to a depth of about 2cm and leave it to set until it is semi-hard (figure 1). Then remove the plaque carefully and incise designs with a pointed tool, such as a nail or compass point (figure 2). Leave it to dry completely, then paint it or rub it with shoe polish and lightly buff it with a soft cloth (figure 3).

Give each child a piece of card and ask them to describe briefly but clearly what is happening in their bas relief. Display each description alongside its plaque.

# Toga time

### Period
Romans.

### Age range
Six to twelve.

### Group size
Individuals or pairs.

### What you need
Pieces of old sheet or other white fabric.

### What to do
The toga was only worn by men who were citizens of Rome. A full-size toga was almost semicircular and about 5.5m (along the straight side) by 2m (at the widest part of the curve).

Figure 1 shows how the toga was put on. Have a child-sized toga ready (about one third smaller than an adult toga) and, using a child as a model, demonstrate to the class how it was worn. Place the straight edge over the left shoulder so that it hangs to the ground in front with the curved side to the outside. Wrap the rest of the toga round behind the body and under the right arm and then throw it over the left shoulder. Take the end hanging down in front of the left shoulder and pull it up under the fold across the body.

Now ask the children to produce their own guide to 'Putting on a toga'. They should all have the opportunity to try putting one on themselves first. Your model can advise the first few and they will soon teach each other. This provides practice in clear, precise instructional writing. Less able children may work best in pairs, putting on a toga and writing about each stage in turn.

The instructions could be accompanied by step-by-step illustrations.

When the children have finished, discuss how the guides might be displayed. You could have a life-sized card figure wearing a fabric toga as a centrepiece, or groups of children could make smaller cardboard figures or clay models (terra cotta coloured clay is appropriate) with fabric togas showing the different stages.

### Follow-up
Examine other clothes that are wrapped rather than cut and sewn, such as saris and turbans.

Present an assembly on the Romans and finish with the whole class putting on togas in unison to a count of three and then marching off.

Figure 1

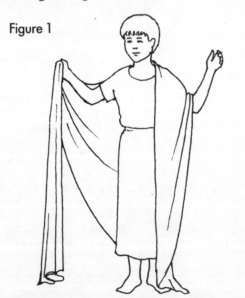  

# Write like the Romans

## Period
Romans.

## Age range
Seven to twelve.

## Group size
Individuals.

## What you need
Pieces of card, wax crayons or oil pastels or black paint and detergent, pieces of cord.

## What to do
Tell the children that, if they had lived in Roman times, they would have written on wax-coated wooden tablets, and explain how they can make their own 'tablets' by putting a paint or crayon surface on to pieces of card. (It is possible to make wax-coated tablets, but it is messy, using up a lot of candle wax, and it is difficult to get an even surface.)

Figure 1

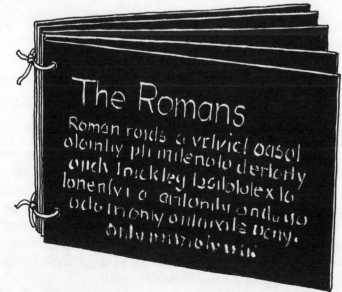

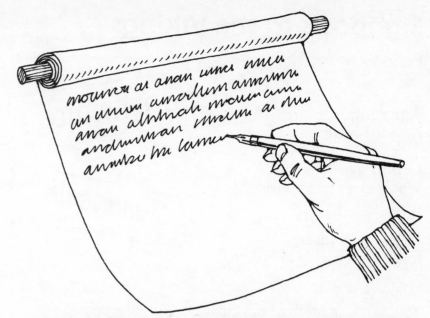

Let the children choose whether to use crayon or paint to coat their card. Mix the black paint with detergent to give a good thick coat, and leave it to dry completely.

They can experiment with various implements to find out which makes the best 'stylus' – this had a pointed end to write with and a blunt end with which to rub out. They could try lolly sticks, sharpened at one end, cocktail sticks or compass points.

The children can try writing information about Roman times on their tablets. Tie the tablets together with pieces of cord to display them (see figure 1); making a 'book' from tablets was a contemporary practice.

Boys who went on to higher education wrote with split reed pens on parchment or papyrus scrolls. Scrolls are easily made by gluing a length of frieze paper to a piece of wooden dowel. Use dip pens and ink to write more about the Romans on the scrolls. The children will discover that referring to a scroll is a much more fiddly business than looking something up in a book.

# Signposts to the Vikings

**Period**
Vikings.

**Age range**
Nine to twelve.

**Group size**
Whole class and individuals.

**What you need**
Maps and atlases,
large outline map of Britain.

**What to do**
Talk to the children about the legacies of the past in our language.

Tell them you are writing some Viking clues on the board – these are the Norse components in our place-names (see box). Who can think of a place-name which contains a Viking clue?

When you have collected all the names that the children can think of, move on to search in maps and atlases (preferably large-scale). First ask the children which parts of the country they think are most likely to have places with names derived from the Vikings. (The north and east.)

**Viking clues:**

| | |
|---|---|
| bie or by = village | garth = dyke or enclosure |
| beck = stream | thwaite = clearing for a farm |
| thorpe = hamlet | dale = valley |
| vik (wick) = bay or inlet | kirk = church |
| | borg (borough) = fort |

Make a large outline map of Britain for the wall on which they can enter a number for each find, with the name on a key alongside.

**Follow-up**
Some of the place-names are a combination of a person's name with 'village' or 'bay', and so on. The children can invent a place-name using their own name combined with a Viking element: eg Anniesthwaite. Ask them to write the story of how the place-name arose, then display these accounts with bold signpost headings.

Talk to the children about how the Vikings settled here and gradually mixed with the Celts and Ango-Saxons, and how their language and culture became part of what was here already. Explain that there are people today who are descendants of those Vikings from long ago – perhaps some of the children are!

*Signpost illustration showing: Samsdale, Hassanthwaite, Petersbeck, Susansvik, Jennythorpe, Helenborg*

# Grave goods

**Period**
Vikings.

**Age range**
Nine to twelve.

**Group size**
Whole class and pairs.

**What you need**
Recording equipment (optional).

**What to do**
Talk about the Viking custom of burying their dead surrounded by all their belongings. The very wealthy Vikings were occasionally buried in their ships.

The Vikings believed that people should not be disturbed in their graves – if they were, they might rise and walk the earth again. So even poor people were buried very thoroughly!

Explain that it is chiefly from these burial customs that our knowledge of the Vikings comes. Ask the children why this is so. (Things buried in the earth are partially preserved from corrosion, rotting and destruction.)

Discuss whether the grave goods may be connected with a belief in life after death.

Suppose we had this custom today. What would the children choose to have buried with them? How many of these things (or parts of them) would survive buried in the earth for more than a thousand years? What might future archaeologists deduce from these grave goods?

The children could answer these questions by imagining they are reporters in the year 3000, and writing a newspaper report of the amazing burial find. Or they could record an interview with an 'archaeological expert'. Would future archaeologists be better informed generally about our times than we are about the Vikings? Why? Might they still misinterpret clues?
Note: Do not choose this activity if you have children in your class who have recently suffered a death in the family or who come from strictly religious homes.

# Writing the runes

### Period
Vikings.

### Age range
Nine to twelve.

### Group size
Individuals.

### What you need
Pictures of Norse designs and runes (writing) from reference books, copies of pages 100–101 for each child, pieces of slate or soft stone, nails, smooth pieces of wood, knives, black, red and white paint, PVC glue.

### What to do
Ask the children to find pictures of Norse runes and designs in the reference books. Point out that most of the Norse designs and writing that still exist are on stone, although it is believed that the Vikings did most of their writing on pieces of wood. Why are so few runes on wood left today?

When the children have studied the pictures, distribute copies of pages 100–101 and ask them to make their own 'Norse' designs and runes. Page 100 shows the Norse alphabet and some Norse inscriptions. Everyone can try copying these or translating them into English letters to find out what they mean using the word list on page 101. Younger and less able children can then go on to scratching their own messages in runes on pieces of slate or stone with a nail, and adding Norse designs like the ones they have seen in the reference books or on page 101.

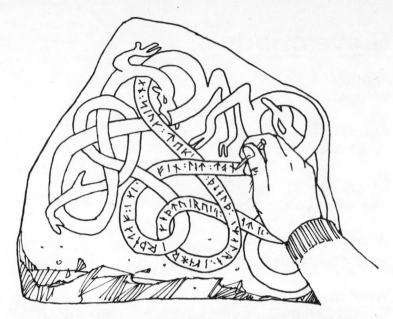

Mix powder paint with PVC glue to paint the designs (don't paint over the runes). Black, red and white were the colours used by the Vikings.

Older children can try transcribing and translating the other runes on the sheet with the help of the Norse-English word list. They could then write messages in runes and even carve their messages on pieces of wood, but only if you are confident in their skill with knives.

### Follow-up
The children could paint pictures or write stories to fill in the background to their messages, explaining who wrote them and why, what happened to the messages to enable them to survive for so many years, and who discovered them. Make a display of the messages and designs, and their accompanying stories and pictures.

Your class may be amused to hear that some runes scratched on stone by primary school children in Orkney were discovered by archaeologists, who were very excited about them, believing them to be genuine!

# Bayeux bas relief

## Period
Norman.

## Age range
Eight to twelve.

## Group size
Pairs.

## What you need
Pieces of expanded polystyrene (tiles or preferably thicker packaging pieces), powder paints, felt-tipped pens, calorettes (night light-type candles), steel knitting needles, pictures from the Bayeux Tapestry.

## What to do
Ask the children to choose a section of the Bayeux Tapestry (a key resource in any study of the Normans) to reproduce in polystyrene bas relief.

First draw the panel shape with a felt-tipped pen on a piece of polystyrene, then draw the chosen scene within the panel. Now the children have to decide which bits of their pictures will be left, and which burned away. (The general rule is that the figures are left, but the background is burned away.) They can mark the bits to be melted with cross-hatching.

Heat the knob-end of a knitting needle in the calorette flame and put it on to the area marked for removal. Move the knob about until it is too cool to melt the polystyrene, and then reheat it. The children may be able to think of alternative implements for this task – the important factor being that it must heat up quickly and allow fairly accurate control. (Make sure the heating process is carefully supervised.)

When the background has been melted away, the relief figures can be painted. Most paints will work on polystyrene. Heat a knife blade (supervised again) to trim off the edge of the panel and provide a neat finish.

This technique can be used for any suitable scene: Viking raids, battles, myths and legends, and so on.

49

# Motte and bailey castle model

## Period
Normans.

## Age range
Nine to eleven.

## Group size
Three or four.

## What you need
For each group: two or three polystyrene tiles, a sharp knife or hot-wire cutter, paints, adhesive, Polyfilla, card, corrugated cardboard.

## What to do
Use one tile as the base of the model and, in one corner, build up a layered motte from circles of polystyrene cut from the other tiles (see figure 1). Glue the motte together and to the base. Mix the Polyfilla to a fairly stiff consistency with green paint and use it to smooth out the steps on the motte. You could add sand for a rougher texture. Draw the net for the keep on card (see figure 2), cut it out, and score, fold and stick it as shown in figure 3. Use corrugated cardboard for the steps to the keep door and the wall enclosing the bailey. The gate and other simple buildings can be cut from card or made from small cardboard boxes.

Figure 2

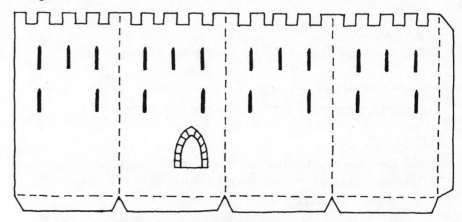

Figure 3

Figure 1

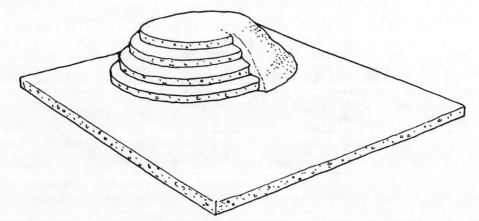

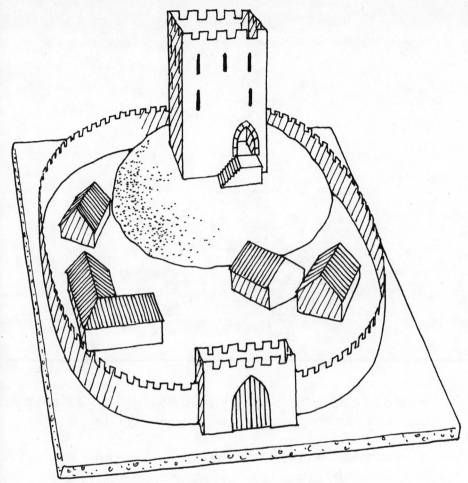

Find as many pictures as possible of motte and bailey castles or photographs of mottes, and display them round your model. Why have none of the castles survived? (They were made of wood.)

## Follow-up
Discuss what the keep would have looked like inside. Children can draw what they would see if the keep was cut in half from top to bottom – use the word 'section'.

# Egg-box knights

## Period
Norman to Middle Ages.

## Age range
Eight to twelve.

## Group size
Individuals or pairs.

## What you need
A number of egg-boxes, small cardboard boxes (about 6cm × 9cm × 2cm), sharp scissors, PVC glue, string, feathers etc, to decorate.

## What to do
Make up a knight or two yourself so that you understand exactly how it is done. Then let the children try to make their own with your models as a guide. Emphasise that yours are only examples, and that they can try different ways of using the pre-formed shapes of the egg-boxes to achieve different effects. They should assemble the parts as they are cut.

Figure 1

Figure 2

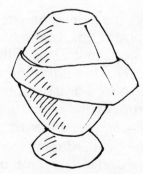

Cut out and trim two cups, and stick them together for the helmet (figure 1, page 51). Cut a cup in half horizontally and glue the top to one end of the helmet to make the neck; the lower part is cut to form the visor and stuck to the helmet (figure 2, page 51).

Figure 5

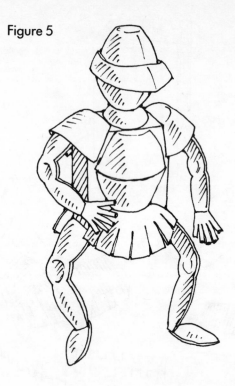

Figure 3          Figure 4

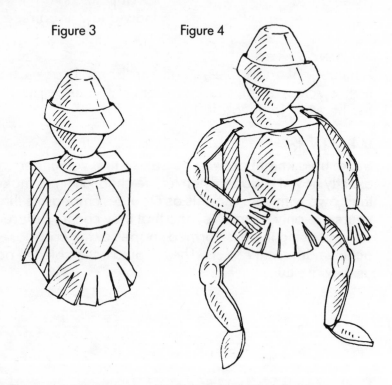

Stick the helmet and neck to one end of the small cardboard box, and build up a breast-plate and skirt on both sides of the box with vertically halved cups, slitting the cup for the skirt (figure 3).

Make legs and arms from cups by cutting up one side of a cup, over the top and down the other side; then glue hands and feet made from scraps to the base of the cups (figure 4). The dent at the top of the cup is the knee or elbow, and the position of the legs and arms can be

varied by cutting them out at different angles. A section of cup stuck to each shoulder completes the knight (figure 5).

The charger is made from the lids of egg-boxes. Cut two head halves from two lids (figure 6) and glue them together. Make eyes and nostrils from the tops of cups,

Figure 6

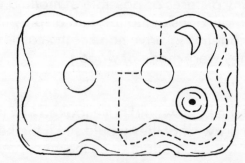

Figure 7

and ears from scraps, then glue the head to a complete lid which forms the charger's body (figure 7).

Cut legs from the tops and sides of more lids, and cut a tail making full use of the curved part of a box (figure 8).

Sit the knight on his charger and add weapons, plumes, and so on, made from scrap material (figure 9). String glued in patterns makes effective decoration.

Figure 8

The rough surface of egg-boxes is difficult to paint, so leave the knights unpainted or use acrylic paints which act as an adhesive and will provide additional support.

Display your knights on a table top and get the children to devise and paint a suitable backdrop to pin to the wall behind the table.

## Follow-up
When the children have looked in reference books to find out about how a boy became a knight, they can name their own knights, write their stories and design suitable devices for their shields (see pages 60–61). Individual knights can then be displayed with their stories alongside them. Foot soldiers and castles could also be made from egg-boxes.

Figure 9

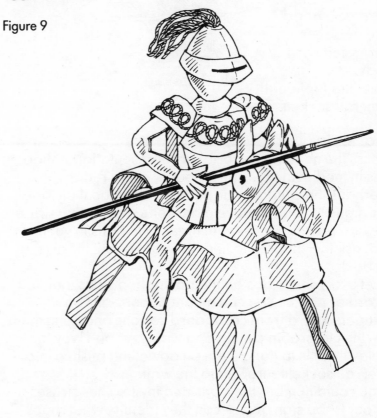

# Shop signs

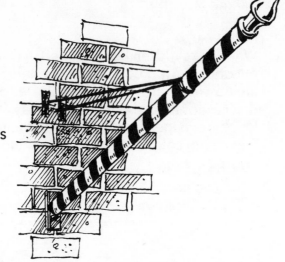

**Period**
Medieval.

**Age range**
Six to twelve.

**Group size**
Individuals or groups
of two or three.

**What you need**
Card or paper,
corrugated card,
paints,
dowelling (optional),
towel rail sockets.

**What to do**
Discuss the need for pictorial or representational shop signs in medieval times (few people could read).

Perhaps the children can think of some local pictorial shop signs. If you still have a barber's shop with a striped pole or a pawnbroker's with three gold balls in your area, ask the children to find out more about these (see fact box).

Get everyone to design their own shop signs, painted on card or paper. You can mount paper signs on corrugated card from cardboard cartons and hang them from the classroom ceiling and walls. A good way to display them is to hang them on dowelling pushed into towel rail sockets screwed to the wall.

You could number the signs and invite other classes to do your 'shop sign quiz' – can they identify what shops the signs belong to?

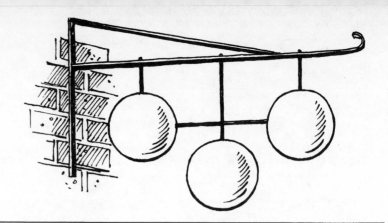

# Fact box
The proliferation of hanging signs in London caused them to be banned in 1762. From then on, shops had the shopkeeper's name and business above the door as they do today. The exceptions to the ban were the pawnbroker's and barber's signs.

The three gold balls of the pawnbroker's sign are said to have been taken from the coat of arms of the Medici family. They were brought to London and used as a sign by the Lombard bankers and money-lenders who were pawnbrokers from the 1200s.

The barber's striped pole is still seen occasionally as a long pole with a gilt knob on the end, but is now more often just a short plastic cylinder. From the Middle Ages to the mid-1700s barbers also acted as surgeons, and the pole is a reminder of blood-letting. Patients gripped a staff – hence the pole; the white spiral reminds us of the bandage that was twisted round the arm before a vein was cut, and the red spiral represents the bandage that was used after the blood-letting. The gilt knob is a reminder of the brass bowl that was fitted under the customer's chin so that he could be lathered before being shaved.

## Follow-up

Even if there are no pictorial shop signs in your area, you are bound to have pub signs. These can lead you into many fascinating areas of local and national history.

Make a collection of local pub names and ask everyone to guess the derivation of these names. Then give each child or group a name to research. They can ask the publican or older residents, look in the local history section in the library or write to the brewery. When they have found out all they can, record the information alongside the original guesses.

Armed with this new knowledge, the children could design suitable signs for those pubs which don't already have pictorial signs. Most publicans would probably be delighted to have the children's work on display inside the pub, together with a clearly written account of the history of the pub's name. (This activity is inappropriate if you have Muslims or children whose parents are strict teetotallers in your class.)

In old towns, you may have street names like Fish Alley, Bakers' Row, and so on. These could indicate streets where, in the past, shops selling the same kinds of goods were grouped together. The children could make some decorative versions of these street name signs for the classroom wall.

# Black letter type

### Period
Middle Ages.

### Age range
Nine to twelve.

### Group size
Pairs.

### What you need
Copies of page 102.

### What to do
This activity can be fitted into work on printing and early books (see also page 59 on illuminated manuscripts).

Give each pair a copy of the black letter type sheet and explain that, in the Middle Ages, this was the typeface used for books in England. (In Germany it was still used until about 50 years ago; you may be able to get hold of some old German books to show the children.)

With the alphabet to help them, ask the children to decipher the message on the sheet. Then they can try writing their own names, or messages for friends to decipher, in black letter type.

## Fact box

In the eleventh century and for some time before, writing was rounded and rather like the Norman architecture of the time. It was known as Carolingian because it was much used by scholars at the court of Charlemagne, whose Latin name was Carolus Magnus.

From the mid-thirteenth century writing grew more pointed and angular, and was complicated with additonal strokes, until it looked rather like the tracery of a church window in the Decorated style. This is called black letter writing.

In the 1400s scholars in Italy rediscovered the Carolingian writing and found it much more attractive and easy to read than black letter writing, so they all took to using it. They called the black letter writing Gothic, which meant 'barbarous'.

Printing in Europe began in Germany where everyone was still writing in black letter, so the printers made their type in that style. The first books printed in Italy were in black letter, perhaps because they were made by German printers who had come to teach the new art, but Italians soon decided to use their new style of writing for printing as well, and they developed the Roman and Italic printing alphabets.

In France and England black letter lasted for a while. In the 1500s and 1600s, books for church use were mostly in black letter, but other books were in Roman and Italic. In the 1600s, some writing masters taught Gothic writing and some Roman but, by the 1700s, black letter was no longer used in England. In Germany it was used until the 1900s and some German books are still printed in black letter.

# What's in a name?

## Period
Middle Ages.

## Age range
Eight to twelve.

## Group size
Whole class.

## What you need
Telephone directories and/or copies of class registers showing surnames.

## What to do
Talk to the children about how, in the Middle Ages, people didn't have surnames inherited from their fathers – they only had first names. However, if there were several people with the same first name in one village, they were given another name to distinguish them. This is how surnames began. These surnames were passed on for seven or eight hundred years.

British surnames today are a direct link with the Middle Ages. They fall into four main categories:
• Names describing occupations: for example, Miller, Weaver, and so on.
• The father's name: Anne Roberts originally meant Anne, belonging to Robert, and Peter Johnson was Peter, son of John. Occasionally a mother's name was used: for example, Mallieson meant Mollie's son.
• The name of the person's place of origin: James Scott would have come from Scotland, and Mary Ford lived near a ford.
• Names about looks or behaviour: examples include Susan Short, Dick Longbottom or Simon Cruikshanks (crooked legs); medieval people weren't always kind with their nicknames!
• Names describing occupations: for example, Miller, Weaver, and so on.

Put a heading for each category on the board, such as 'Whose child?', 'Where from?', 'What are they like?' and 'What do they do?' See how many of the children's surnames will fit one of the categories, then ask them to think of other names which might fit. Finally, look at names in the telephone directories or class registers, but don't expect to be able to categorise every name.

Look out for names describing colour – not only Grey, White, Brown, Black (and Blake), but also derivations of these. A blonde person might also have been called Snow, Frost, Swan or Lilley. Redheads were called Reed, Reid or Raede – what does this tell us about medieval spelling?

Why are some names so common? Why do we have so many Smiths, Millers and Bakers?

Using the telephone directory, the children can compile a list of the most common medieval trades. Remind them again that spellings have changed: for example, Taylor is the old spelling for Tailor. Medieval tailors made all kinds of clothes, including shoes, so no-one has Shoemaker as a surname, although in Germany, where surnames began at a later date, Schumacher and Schumann are common.

Ask the children to think about the names Skinner, Tanner and Barker. What did these people do and why were they important? (The tanner used bark to prepare the skins.) Walker is common because he trampled woven cloth under running water to clean and soften it.

## Whose child?
Peterson
Richardson
Jamieson

## Where from?
York
Scott
Rivers

## What are they like?
Rich Long Short

## What do they do?
Cooper Mason Weaver
Miller Smith

The Welsh were late in establishing second names and nearly all of them originate with the first names: ap-William (son of William) developed into Williams, and ap-John became Jones. Sometimes, if the first name began with R or H, the 'p' from 'ap' was attached to the surname: for example, ap-Richard became Pritchard, ap-Harry became Parry, and so on.

In the Highlands 'mac' meant 'son of' or 'descendant of', which explains the great number of surnames beginning with Mac and Mc. The children only have to look in the telephone directory again to see how common these names are.

In Ireland we find more Macs and many names beginning with 'O', such as O'Neill, O'Connor and O'Brian, where 'O' means 'of'. (Niall, Conar and Brian were three Kings in early Irish history.) Irish surnames are very old, many dating back to the tenth century.

Transfer your blackboard list to sheets of paper fixed to the wall, so that children can add more names (with explanations if necessary) as they think of them or come across them.

The children could use the largest dictionary available to trace old meanings of words, but the word must be designated as OE (Old English) or ME (Middle English), since more recent words would not have formed

surnames. They may also find *How Surnames Began* by C M Matthews (Butterworth) and *The Dictionary of British Surnames* by P H Reaney (Routledge & Kegan Paul) very useful.

Ask the children why we don't have people called Postman, Electrician or Engine-Driver. This will remind them of the early origins of our names.

Finally, get them to invent names for themselves which will fit one of the four categories. (The occupational ones could be whatever they want to do when they grow up.) Write these names on the board and ask the children to put them into alphabetical order. Use this list for calling the register for as long as it amuses you and them!

## Follow-up
Because this activity is linked to work on the Middle Ages, you will inevitably be looking at British surnames but you could go on to look at how the naming systems of other cultures originated. For example, Sikh men are all called Singh which means 'lion', and Sikh women are called Kaur, meaning 'princess'; Chinese names are in reverse order with the family names first, and so on.

David Elmtrees

Joanna Crossroads

Susan Computer-Programmer

Jason Garyson

Patti Sarasgirl

Ahmad Doctor

Lucy Longlegs

Peter Busstop

Tony Goggles

Keim Engineer

Jasminder Pilot

Ann Kevinschild

Bimla Pigtails

Renuka Weatherforecaster

Simon Rollerskates

# Illuminated manuscripts

**Period**
Middle Ages.

**Age range**
Nine to twelve.

**Group size**
Individuals.

**What you need**
Good quality white paper (preferably browned in a slow oven for a 'parchment' effect), quill or dip pens, black ink, coloured inks (including gold if possible) and fine brushes or coloured felt-tipped pens, pictures of illuminated manuscripts (preferably in colour), copies of page 103.

**What to do**
When the children have done some writing in rough about the Middle Ages, show them the pictures of illuminated manuscripts and copies of page 103, then suggest that they present their work in this way.

Tell them about the monks who did this beautiful work in the days before printing, when all books were copied out by hand and were very precious.

An alternative to writing out their own work would be to illuminate their black letter writing (see pages 55–56) or a piece of writing taken from the Middle Ages – for example, a verse from the 'Cuckoo Song' (c 1226):

Sumer is icumen in,
Lhude sing cuccu!
Groweth sed, and bloweth med,
And springeth the wude nu –
        Sing cuccu!

or a piece from Chaucer's prologue to the *Canterbury Tales* (c 1367):

A Knight ther was, and that a worthy man,
That from the tyme that he ferst bigan
To ryden out, he lovede chyvalrye,
Trouthe and honour, fredom and curtesie.

The lines for the writing and the space to be occupied by the illumination should be sketched out first on a piece of rough paper of the right size. Slow workers can write a short piece with just an illuminated capital, while the more able can tackle a whole illuminated page.

The writing in black should be done first with the outline of the capital and any other decoration pencilled in, and the illumination added in colour afterwards. If the children have seen some good reproductions of the real thing, they should be able to produce their own versions without too much guidance from you.

Felt-tipped pens are easier to use, but coloured inks will give the best effect. The outline of the illustration should be done finely in black and then filled in with the inks. Each colour must be left to dry before another is used.

# Coat of arms

## Period
Middle Ages.

## Age range
Eight to twelve.

## Group size
Individuals.

## What you need
Paints or crayons or felt-tipped pens, copies of pages 104–105, templates of shield shapes (trace the one around the fact box), books on heraldry, a local coat of arms.

## What to do
Talk about how coats of arms started in the Middle Ages (see fact box on page 61), and explore the background to a local coat of arms – the school's, the town's, a local noble family's or a pub's. Ask the children to look out for more coats of arms and, if possible, to bring copies of them to school. When you have looked at several examples and perhaps made a display of them with as much information as possible, suggest that the children design their own coat of arms.

Distribute copies of pages 104–105 and go through it with them. They can colour in the shield and discuss with each other what they might put on their own shields (it could refer to their name or something special about where they live, or it might show the occupation of someone in their family). Have some cardboard templates of shield shapes ready (see fact box). The size of the template can be determined by how much space you have to display the finished shields, and whether you are using paints (suitable for larger shields), felt-tipped pens or crayons. Ask the children to do their designs in rough first and check them to make sure the rules about colours have been observed. (There is no need for rough designs to be fully coloured in; they can be labelled for colours or have sample patches on them.)

Some children may need help with ideas for their shields. Encourage them to look at lots of examples in the heraldry books, and talk to them about their families, interests, and so on.

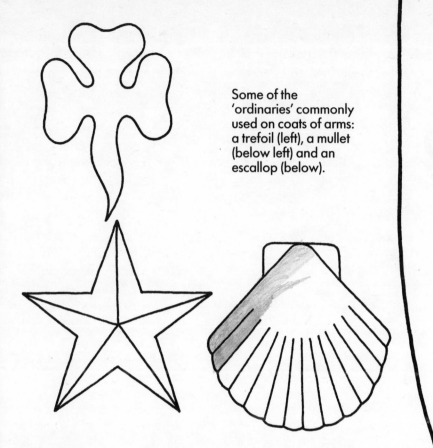

Some of the 'ordinaries' commonly used on coats of arms: a trefoil (left), a mullet (below left) and an escallop (below).

## Follow-up

Write mottos to display beneath the shields. Some children could try, with the help of the heraldry books, to write the blazon (formal description) of their shields. Others could make pennons – the triangular flags carried by knights on their lances – with their devices on. Devices can also be displayed on model knights (see pages 51–53).

If your school hasn't a coat of arms, you could devise one, or you could expand the school shield into a full achievement (coat of arms), with helmet, crest, mantle, supporters, and so on.

## Fact box

In battles and tournaments it was difficult to recognise knights, hidden in their armour, and so, from about 1066, it became customary for a knight to wear an identifying device or coat of arms. These were initially very simple – a bar or cross, or a single animal in bright colours. But as more and more families assumed arms, they had to become more complicated to avoid duplication. In 1484 the College of Arms was founded and strict rules about coats of arms were laid down by the heralds, who still control the carrying of arms today.

Heraldry has its own language – a mixture of Latin, Norman-French and early English. Some older children may enjoy using the technical terms of heraldry to blazon their designs.

The surface of the shield is called the field. This can be charged (decorated) in various ways by ordinaries (bands or stripes). Other decorations can be added and these are known as charges.

Only certain colours and patterns can be used in heraldry, which are listed on the copy sheet. When choosing the colours for the field and charges of a coat of arms, you must not put a colour on a colour, or a metal on a metal, or a fur on a fur.

A complete coat of arms is called an achievement and is very complex. It is built round the shield (escutcheon). At the top there is the crest, resting on a wreath, cap or coronet, which lies on top of the helmet (differing in style depending on the rank). Mantling hangs from the helmet, on either side of the shield there are supporters (people or animals) and below the shield is the motto.

61

# Tudor to
# Victorian

# Horn books

## Period
Fifteenth to nineteenth centuries.

## Age range
Seven to twelve.

## Group size
Three or four.

## What you need
Copies of page 106, wood offcuts (about 30cm × 15cm) or stout cardboard, pieces of acetate, 'parchment' (paper browned in a slow oven), black ink, dip or quill pens (see page 26), adhesive, tacks or drawing-pins, gold sticky tape or ribbon (optional).

## What to do
Explain to the children that, long ago, when books were rare and expensive, children were not able to have real books of their own to learn to read. Instead they had horn books. Get the children to find out what these were, using reference books (see fact box on page 64).

When the research is complete, give each child a copy of page 106. Referring to this and any other pictures they have found, help them to make their own horn books in the following way.

Cut a paddle shape from a suitable offcut of wood. (Younger children could use cardboard.) Cut a sheet of 'parchment' to fit the board. (See figure 1.)

After practising on rough paper to get the spacing right, use a dip or quill pen to write the alphabet, vowels and Lord's Prayer as shown on the copy sheet.

Stick the parchment to the board, cut a piece of acetate to cover it, then pin or tack the acetate to the board. The horn was often kept in place by a brass strip, as shown on the sheet, so use gold sticky tape or ribbon to represent the strip. (See figure 2.)

Figure 1

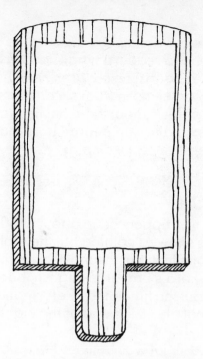

Figure 2

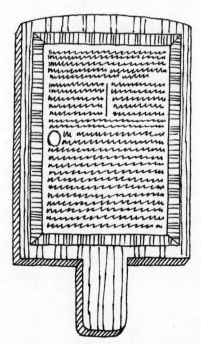

When the books are finished, discuss the differences between learning to read from horn books and learning from the reading books the children have used. Then make a display of the horn books, collate everything the children know or feel about them on the blackboard, and write up the information on a large horn-book shape to form the centrepiece of the display.

## Fact box

Horn books first appeared in about 1450. The earliest ones showed nothing but the alphabet, later some had Latin text, but the most usual form, showing the Lord's Prayer in English, became common about the time of the Reformation and continued until about the end of the eighteenth century.

The printed sheet was fastened to a bat-shaped piece of wood and then covered by a thin sheet of horn, held in place by an edging strip which was usually made of brass. The true horn book (including the sheet of horn) was only used in England and America. No record has been found of its use anywhere else, although the sheets for the English books were often printed in Holland, France and Italy.

Virtually all the surviving horn books are those designed for teaching reading, although one or two versions with sheets of writing samples, fixed to iron plates and covered with horn, remain.

A fescue or pointer was often used to point to the words or letters on the horn book. This might have been a straw, a pin, a pen, a quill, a feather or a piece of wood or bone, held by the child or the teacher.

# Pedlar dolls

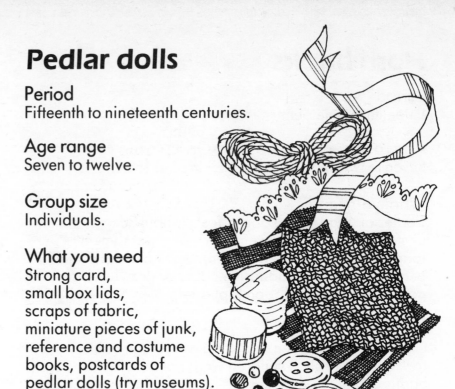

**Period**
Fifteenth to nineteenth centuries.

**Age range**
Seven to twelve.

**Group size**
Individuals.

**What you need**
Strong card, small box lids, scraps of fabric, miniature pieces of junk, reference and costume books, postcards of pedlar dolls (try museums).

**What to do**
Check all the reference books for any mention or pictures of pedlars and have these to hand, together with books from the library if possible.

Talk to the children about communications and shopping in the period you are studying. How did people who lived in the country do their shopping? There were no buses or cars, poorer people couldn't afford a horse, mail order didn't exist – in fact, people had to be very much more self-sufficient than we are today.

A trip to a town to shop would happen only very occasionally, possibly at one of the annual fairs, and was something to be looked forward to, planned for months in advance and talked about long afterwards. The pedlars who walked the country with a pack of wares on their backs were the nearest thing to a travelling shop that existed, and they would have received a much warmer welcome from country people than travelling salesmen do today. (Why are travelling salesmen nowadays found chiefly in towns?)

Pedlar dolls were popular toys throughout Europe in the eighteenth and nineteenth centuries. Show the children the postcards of pedlar dolls, and suggest that they make their own dolls, which could be dressed according to the period you are working on.

Cut the basic doll shape from stout card, paint it or make clothes from scraps of fabric, and staple a small box lid to the front of the doll and a support to the back (see figure 1).

Figure 1

The fun starts with devising the miniature items for the tray, and a lot of research and learning goes into deciding what the pedlars might have carried. Fabric can be cut up to make bolts of cloth, ribbon and scarves. Should synthetic fabric be used? Beads and bottle tops can be used for saucepans and other utensils. What sort of plates and cups did they use? People would also need scissors, knives and needles. When were scissors invented?

A very valuable service performed by the pedlars for their customers, who never saw a bookshop or a library, was to sell chapbooks. These little 24-page books were crudely abridged and cheaply printed versions of favourite books of the time, or classic legends and stories, and they reached a wide audience through the pedlars, who were sometimes called chapmen. What stories might your pedlar have in his or her chapbooks?

# Elizabethan houses

## Period
Tudor.

## Age range
Six to twelve.

## Group size
Two or three.

## What you need
Cardboard boxes of various sizes, card, white paint, PVC glue, yellow tissue-paper, match-sticks, ice-lolly sticks or balsa wood, wood dye, natural raffia, modelling clay, illustrations and pictures of half-timbered houses.

## What to do
When the children have studied some pictures of Elizabethan houses (or better still, visited, sketched and photographed a local Elizabethan building), they can make model houses. Two cuboids of slightly different sizes are needed as the basis for the models. Older children can make their own cuboids by drawing nets on card first (remember to cut out the windows and doors before making up the cuboids).

Figure 1

Figure 2

Glue the larger cuboid on top of the smaller one to give the overhang or 'jetty'. Paint the cuboids white, then stain the match-sticks, ice-lolly sticks or strips of balsa wood with wood dye before gluing the timber framing in place.

Draw diamond panes with black felt-tipped pens on pieces of tissue-paper, and glue these to the inside of the window spaces (figure 1). Why did houses of this period have panes like these? (It was too difficult and expensive to make large sheets of glass.)

Make a prism from card for the roof (or cut a box in half diagonally). Glue the roof to the top cuboid, thatch it with raffia and add a modelling-clay chimney after discussing the shape of Elizabethan chimneys (figure 2).

Add the glow of candle-light by placing small bulbs and batteries behind the windows. Make sure that everyone realises these represent candle-light, rush dips or oil lamps and not electricity!

The children could build up a whole Elizabethan street with these models, including shops with signs hanging outside (see pages 54–55). They can decide who the occupants of their houses were and devise biographies for them, elaborating their models accordingly.

# Reading a historical document

## Period
Sixteenth century.

## Age range
Nine to twelve.

## Group size
Pairs.

## What you need
Copies of page 107 or 108.

## What to do
Give each pair of children a copy of one of the historical document sheets. Sheet 1 is of general interest, while sheet 2 is more suitable if you have done some work on the religious controversy of the period and the persecution of Catholics.

Explain that the documents from which these extracts are taken are some of those used by historians to build up a picture of life in the past.

Get them to read the piece, giving them as little help as possible. If someone is stuck, ask the other children if they can help. They will probably work out that 'ye' means 'the', but the small 'j's at the end of Roman numerals on sheet 1 may defeat them – these are simply another 'i', since the final 'i' was written as 'j'. Reading aloud will help with strange-looking words.

Then discuss the passage. They both come from the *Historical Memoranda* written by a chronicler called John Stowe in the sixteenth century. What do the children think of the spelling? Did anyone notice that it is inconsistent? (For example, there are two different spellings of 'gun powder' and 'moon' on sheet 1.) The hotchpotch of events on sheet 1 is typical of many early historical documents.

Sheet 2 will give you a further opportunity to discuss the importance of religion in the past and the violent feelings that were aroused between Protestant and Catholic in the sixteenth century. Can the children think of anywhere today where feelings about religion are equally strong? (Northern Ireland, the Middle East and Asia.)

Work out a modern translation together and write it on the board.

# Biblical English

### Period
Seventeenth century.

### Age range
Nine to twelve.

### Group size
Individuals or pairs.

### What you need
Copies of authorised (King James) version of the Bible, New English Bible, Good News Bible or other modern translation, reference books on seventeenth century.

### What to do
What was seventeenth century English like? Tell the children that we have a very good example of seventeenth century English in a book which many people know well today. See if they can guess that it is the Bible.

They can use reference books to find out more about how the Bible came to be written, and why the authorised version is called the King James Bible. Follow up this work with research into the history of writings from other religions, such as the Koran.

The children could choose a part of the Bible to translate into modern English. Suggest the following: *Psalm* 23, *Psalm* 121, *Samuel* I 17 vv4–10 and vv32–51 (David and Goliath), *Genesis* I vv1–31 (the creation), *Exodus* 14 vv19–30 (the parting of the Red Sea), *Job* 39 vv19–25, *Luke* 10 vv25–37 (the good Samaritan), *Luke* 15 vv1–7 (the parable of the lost sheep), *Corinthians* I 13 vv1–13. A concordance or dictionary of quotations may be helpful in tracking down a particular piece a child has chosen.

When they have written their translations (they may find this easier to do in pairs), give them the Good News or New English Bible, or another modern translation, so that they can read their passage in modern English.

Read out some of the versions to the class — the authorised version, the child's translation and the modern Bible version. Which do they prefer? (Point out that there is no right answer to this question — it is simply a matter of taste.)

# Union Jack

### Period
Seventeenth century to
early nineteenth century.

### Age range
Nine to twelve.

### Group size
Two or three and individuals.

### What you need
Reference books with
pictures of flags,
copies of pages 109 and 110,
red and blue crayons
or felt-tipped pens,
scissors.

### What to do
Ask the children to draw the Union Jack from memory.
Few children are likely to be able to do this successfully.

Get them to do some research and find out the basic
facts about the flag's history (see fact box on page 70).
What is its significance? How long has it existed in its
present form?

When the research is done, distribute copies of pages
109 and 110. Page 109 shows the three saints' flags then
the first Union flag, the Commonwealth flag with the
harp, and the Union Jack. These can be coloured in and
stuck into the children's books for reference.

Page 110 shows the three saints' flags again. When
these are coloured in, cut out along the dotted lines and
superimposed upon each other, the children will be able
to see quite clearly how the Union Jack is made up.

Explain that the flag flown upside-down is a signal of
distress, so it is important to know the right way to fly the
Union Jack (with the broader white stripe uppermost
nearest the flag-pole). When do we fly flags at half-mast?
(To mourn the death of a famous person or deaths in a
disaster.)

### Follow-up
Design a school flag and make it up from fabric, or make
a class Union Jack and find out more about the three
saints whose crosses are shown on the flag.

Investigate the history of other flags, particularly for
countries with which children in your class have
connections.

## Fact box

A jack is a small flag flown by a ship to show her nationality. In the Middle Ages, English ships flew a flag with the cross of St George, and Scottish ships had one with the white 'saltire' cross of St Andrew on a blue background.

When James I of England (James VI of Scotland) came to rule over both countries, he had the two flags united in the Union flag in 1606.

During the Civil War, the union was for a time dissolved, and the ships returned to the two original jacks. In 1649, Cromwell introduced the Commonwealth Jack which combined the St George cross with the harp of Ireland. When Charles II came back to the throne in 1660 he reintroduced the Union flag. The flag in this form remained until 1801 when Ireland was incorporated into the union of Great Britain and the cross of St Patrick was added to make the Union Jack as we know it.

Cross of St George     Cross of St Andrew

Commonwealth Jack     Cross of St Patrick

# Post time

### Period
Seventeenth to nineteenth centuries.

### Age range
Seven to twelve.

### Group size
Individuals.

### What you need
Sheets of paper browned in a slow oven, candles or candle ends (preferably red), coins or decorative metal buttons with a relief surface to act as seals, quill pens (see page 26) or ink pens, black or brown ink, used envelopes of various shapes and sizes.

### What to do
Get the children to do some research into the history of the postal service. Try your local Post Office, and there is further information in the fact box.

Then ask them to calculate how long it would have taken a letter to travel from London to Edinburgh (400 miles) in the 1600s when the post took 24 hours to cover 120 miles. In the 1700s, the post took 42 hours to reach Edinburgh from London — how fast was it travelling then? How long does it take today?

In 1797 postal charges rose sharply (see fact box). It cost the equivalent of four pennies to send a single sheet 15 miles — what effect would this have on what people wrote and how they wrote it? (A working man's average wage was about ten shillings, or 120 pennies, a week.)

The class could make graphs showing the rise and fall of postal rates from the seventeenth century to the present day, and decorate them with illustrations of stamps from different periods.

Ask the children to try writing 'eighteenth century' letters using browned paper and quill or ink pens.

Envelopes did not come into general use until the introduction of the penny post, so space had to be left for the address when the sheet was folded and sealed.

Fold the letters so that the open edge can be sealed. Drip wax from a lighted candle carefully on to this edge and seal it by pressing the coin or button into the wax while it is still warm. Add a signature to frank the letter. Give one used envelope to each child and ask them to

draw the net which will make that envelope. Then they can unstick their envelope to see whether their net is the right shape. Discuss the advantages of using an envelope.

## Fact box

In the Middle Ages, universities and guilds of merchants had private postal services. In 1597 legislation was introduced to control postal services as a security measure against foreign agents. Letters sent abroad were to be conveyed only by messengers organised by the master of the posts. In 1609 inland letters came under the same rule.

In 1635 Thomas Witherings reorganised the postal services and made them a source of revenue instead of a charge on the Crown. His posts travelled by night and day out of London on the post roads to the post towns. Subsidiary posts radiated from the post towns. Charges for a single sheet were:
up to 80 miles – two pennies;
80–140 miles – four pennies;
more than 140 miles – six pennies;
borders and Scotland – nine pennies.

At the end of the 1700s improved roads allowed for rapid stage coaches, which were faster than the post boys on horse-back. By 1797, 42 mail coach routes were in operation, all leaving London at 8 pm. Postal rates were increased to obtain revenue for the war with France. In 1836, the high postal rates were still in force and Rowland Hill suggested the idea of a penny post, regardless of distance. This was put into operation in 1840, and stamps for prepayment were introduced. Penny postage on inland letters lasted until the end of World War I.

# Change of clothes

**Period**
Victorian.

**Age range**
Seven to twelve.

**Group size**
Individuals or groups of four or five.

**What you need**
Copies of page 111.

## What to do

Ask the children to tell you anything they can about the objects shown on the sheet. They will probably be able to guess that the machine is a sewing machine, but they are unlikely to recognise the buttonhook or glove stretchers.

The machine shown is a very early sewing machine (1871). Commercial machines were first used in American factories in about 1850, and home machines soon followed.

Ask the children to look at something they are wearing and examine the machine stitching. Hand stitches made by a good seamstress would have been almost as close together as machine stitches, and were even in size.

In eary Victorian times, all girls and women, except rich ones, had to do a tremendous amount of sewing to make their families' clothes. Men's coats and trousers might be bought from a tailor, but everything else had to be sewn or knitted at home, and sheets, towels, tablecloths and handkerchiefs were all hemmed by hand. Rich women had their clothes made by a dressmaker. Even little girls of four or five learned to sew very neatly, and by the time

they were seven or eight they could make themselves frocks and pinafores. Why did so many Victorian children wear pinafores? (Their clothes were made of materials which were not easily washed, and a pinafore protected them.)

When they were learning to sew, little girls very often made a sampler, which usually showed the alphabet, their name and age, and sometimes a rhyme or proverb.

Discuss the difference between the children's clothes and those worn by Victorian children. Did the Victorians have zips, elastic or nylon? (Zips date back to about 1925, elastic was not used in clothing until after World War I, except for hat elastic and elastic-sided boots, and synthetic materials were not common until after World War II.) How did they fasten and hold up their clothes without zips and elastic? (They used buttons, hooks and eyes, and tapes.)

Get the children to analyse their clothes, then try to imagine what it would be like to wear woollen underwear, bodices with stockings buttoned to them, flannel petticoats and stiff, heavy clothes, all fastened with tapes, hooks and eyes, and buttons.

Look at some Victorian photographs. What were their bathing suits like? Everyone wore hats, caps and bonnets, and boots were commonly worn instead of shoes. Women's boots were often buttoned, which brings in the second object on the sheet – a button hook which was used to help fasten the boot buttons.

Gloves were an essential part of any lady's outfit. Fine ladies wore kid leather gloves which were tight when new, so the ivory glove-stretchers shown on the sheet were used to stretch the gloves before they were worn.

With the help of old photographs and costume reference books, the children could draw Victorian children alongside modern children in underclothes and in top clothes, with captions and arrows pinpointing the differences. Some children might like to try making cardboard figures which could be dressed in paper clothes held on by tabs folded over the shoulders. Alternatively, they could work in groups to make life-sized figures for the classroom wall.

During the Victorian period (1830–1900), there were many changes of fashion for children as well as adults, and no one style is typical of the whole period, so the children should label their illustrations with a precise date.

They should also be aware of the great differences between the clothes worn by prosperous people – depicted in most costume reference books – and the very basic ragged garments, with no pretensions to current fashion, worn by the poor. (Look at some contemporary photographs of slums.) Poor children never had new clothes and were frequently dressed in adults' clothes which were threadbare and cut down to size. Is there such a great difference between the clothes of rich and poor people today? Why not? (There are higher living standards and greater affluence for everyone, more state support for the poor, and cheap, mass-produced clothes.)

# Victorian classroom

**Period**
Victorian.

**Age range**
Eight to eleven.

**Group size**
Whole class.

**What you need**
Copies of pages
112–118, a slate
(try builders'
merchants or
demolition sites)
dip pens,
ink.

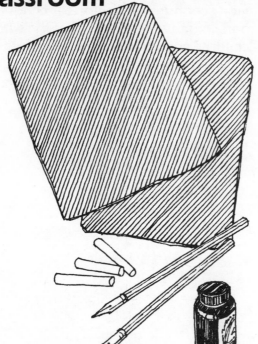

**What to do**
Here are some ideas for one aspect of the kind of drama
and role-play discussed on page 11. It is obviously more

effective in a Victorian building, but even in a modern
building you can do quite a lot to set the scene.

Put all the desks in rows facing yours, and place yours
up on a dais if you can (perhaps a stage block from the
hall). Cover the lower parts of the windows with paper
painted like brickwork so that no-one can see out, and
take down pictures and displays of work. Someone may
have a Victorian (or repro) school clock you can borrow,
and a picture of Queen Victoria or an old map or
Victorian engraving which you could hang on the walls.
Failing that, you could write out and display a saying (see
page 112). Ask the local museum or library services if
they can provide suitable books or objects.

74

## Clothes

Everyone must dress up as far as possible, including you. There are some ideas for costume on page 8. Boys could have plain dark sweaters or jackets, shorts or dark trousers tucked into long socks coming above the knee (for knickerbocker suits), and heavy shoes or boots. Eton collars can be made from stiff white paper, and adults' worn-out trousers can be cut down for anyone wanting to be a poor boy. Encourage them to get their hair cut (short back and sides)! Girls need dark dresses with full skirts and white pinafores if they can make them, black tights (which would have been stockings) and heavy shoes or boots. Long hair can be tied back with a bow.

## Lessons

Seat the children in alphabetical order of surname – boys on one side of the class and girls on the other – or alternate rows of boys and girls. Start by having the class stand up and greet you respectfully in unison: 'Good morning, (your name).' Respond with 'Good morning children', and give them a steely look before saying 'You may be seated.'

Make sure they sit up very straight – get them to clasp their hands behind their backs and pull them down to achieve the right posture. Strictly enforce a rule of no talking – if anyone disobeys, bark at them 'Hands on heads!' and make them sit like that for a while.

You might start the lesson by getting them to chant some tables in unison. Then give them a tables test, with answers being written on slates or long strips of paper with dip pens. The children could wrestle with the mysteries of old money as they try the maths problems on pages 113–115. Then you could do some 'drill' – exercises in unison while you count 'One! Two! Three! Four!' Then settle down to some handwriting practice using dip pens to copy the elevating sentiments on page 112.

These sentences were taken from a child's copybook of 1852 – they were each copied ten times to fill a whole page of unlined paper.

While the children are doing their writing, you could put up a list of countries and their capitals on the board. Once again, these can be recited in unison several times. Tell the children to sit in silence and learn the capitals, then clean the blackboard and test them.

Finish off with a poetry recitation, such as 'The Village Blacksmith' or 'The Wreck of the Hesperus' (both by Longfellow) – see pages 116–118. You could divide the class into groups (with a good reader in each group), and ask each group to read a different verse or verses in turn. (There are suggestions on how to divide up 'The Wreck of the Hesperus' for four groups.) If the children enjoy reading the poetry aloud, they could learn their verse or verses and try reciting rather than reading (with a lot of emphasis and dramatic gestures). This recitation could be used in a 'Victorian' assembly.

Try to maintain the atmosphere of sternness and don't allow the children to speak unless they are spoken to, but watch out for children who may become distressed if you are too unlike your normal self. If an adult comes into the room, make sure they know that they must stand up and stay standing silently until they are told they may sit down. At break they could play some of the games they have learned about (see pages 80–81).

The emphasis should be on learning by rote, keeping quiet, doing exactly as they are told, neatness and order. At the end of the day, discuss the experiences, and explain that a Victorian class would probably have been very much larger. Don't be surprised if some children think Victorian ways are preferable to modern ones! For some quiet or insecure children the silence and discipline is a restful change.

Point out that you haven't carried realism to the point of hitting their knuckles with a ruler, caning them or sitting them in a corner in a dunce's cap if they got their sums wrong. Most children won't even know the word 'dunce', so you will have to explain this unpleasant custom.

76

# Blades of steel

**Period**
Pre-1918 with particular reference to Victorians and Edwardians.

**Age range**
Nine to eleven.

**Group size**
Individuals.

**What you need**
Copies of page 119, bright new nails (the larger the better, preferably flat-sided), small dishes.

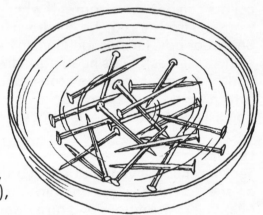

**What to do**
Make sure that every child has a copy of the illustration on page 119, then ask for ideas. What is it?

It is unlikely that any child will know, so they will need a lot of hints (see fact box).

When you have reached a conclusion, talk about the difficulties of keeping blades bright before the invention of stainless steel. Give each child a nail to put into a dish of water, then put these to one side for as long as possible – the nails will become rusty within about a week. Allow them to dry and then the children can experiment with ways of cleaning them. Make sure they take great care not to cut themselves on the rusty nails.

They will probably suggest domestic household cleaners first, but encourage them to realise that what they need is some sort of abrasive material. Ask them to think of other rough objects. Stones, bricks, sand, sandpaper, steel wool, emery paper, and so on, can all be tried.

Newly formed rust is easier to clean off than established rust, so find some older pieces of rusted metal for them to work on, too.

Which abrasives work best, and which make the least mess? Encourage the children to write about their experiments and their conclusions.

## Follow-up
Ask the children to think of some common everyday object which, if shown to children in 100 years' time, might puzzle them due to its obsolescence. What guesses might these children make as to its uses?

## Fact box
The object shown on page 119 is a Victorian knife machine, used for cleaning steel table knives. Stainless steel was not in common use until about 1920 and steel knives became stained and rusty if they were not regularly cleaned.

This machine would have been used in a large Victorian or Edwardian household, probably every day. The knives fitted into the slots with some knife powder (an abrasive powder), and the handle was turned so that brushes inside cleaned the blades.

This would probably have been the kitchen maid's or 'tweeny's' job, but it might have been done by the outside man. In a larger household, it would have been the boot boy's job, as in the illustration. In simpler households, knives were cleaned by rubbing them on a knife board with emery powder, or on a doorstep. Keeping domestic, working and fighting blades clean has been a preoccupation for thousands of years. Egyptians are believed to have used iron as early as 3000 BC.

# The twentieth century

# What was it like when you were young?

### Period
First half of the twentieth century.

### Age range
Eight to twelve.

### Group size
Individuals.

### What you need
Copies of page 120.

### What to do
Talk to the children about their memories of the past. Discuss how these memories make up history, although it is comparatively recent. Ask them to think of any new inventions or significant changes during their lifetime (such as the use of light pens to read bar codes for pricing in shops).

Talk about how different things may be when they are old and their children and grandchildren are growing up, and how their memories will be very much a part of history to young people. Older or more able children may be able to imagine and write a conversation which might take place in the future, between themselves and their grandchildren.

Now suggest that they talk to the oldest person they know and ask him or her about their memories of the past. Draw up a list of questions to be answered. (If they suggest unsuitable questions, discuss why they are not acceptable rather than rejecting them out of hand.)

Compare your questions with the ones on the sheet (page 120). You could add to the list on the sheet or adapt it, but you may decide to discard it and duplicate your own if it is very different.

Unless the children have access to a tape-recorder, they will have to learn note-making skills. Discuss the problem of writing and listening at the same time and how much they need to write. They could practise the questionnaire on you, asking questions in turn with everyone making notes. Poor writers will find this difficult, so explain that only key words, dates, and so on, need to be noted.

Prepare the children for some of the problems they may encounter, like refusal to answer a question, and make sure they know how to handle these situations politely. They need to understand that the questionnaire is only a framework and not a strait-jacket – they mustn't miss out on a fascinating story simply because it isn't an answer to one of the listed questions.

When the children have completed their interviews, they can write up an account of what they have heard using their notes. Less able writers could report back verbally or on tape.

When everyone pools their findings, you may come across conflicting evidence. Discuss the possible reasons for this. Were the respondents of different ages? Did they live in the same area or earn the same sort of income? (You need to be tactful here if children have been interviewing relatives.)

Finish off the work by compiling a class book on 'What We Learned About 19— to 19—.'

If one of the children has found a particularly lively and interesting contact, try to arrange for this person to come in and talk to the class, and make a recording of what he or she says.

# Games time

### Period
Twentieth century (and earlier).

### Age range
Eight to twelve.

### Group size
Whole class.

### What you need
*Children's Games in Street and Playground* Iona and Peter Opie (Oxford).

### What to do
This activity links with 'What was it like when you were young?' (see pages 79–80), since a question on games is included in the questionnaire for old people.

Children are very interested to find out what games their parents, grandparents and elderly relatives played, and to pinpoint similarities and differences. They will be equally fascinated by *Children's Games in Street and Playground* by Iona and Peter Opie, in which they can look up the games they have heard about and find out more about their origins and regional differences.

Suggest that they compile their own book of current and older rhymes and games. They may well find that they have discovered a game that doesn't appear in the Opie book. Encourage them to see this as a piece of genuine historical research, and to be meticulous about acquiring and recording relevant detail: for example, dates, places and explanations of local references.

There is plenty of historical detail in children's rhymes and games. Well beyond World War II, little girls were still chanting a ball-against-the-wall rhyme which ended

'turn your back on the Kaiser'. Are there any current rhymes which have similar references, which people in the future may need an explanation for?

Encourage the children to sing the songs, chant the rhymes and play the games they have collected. This may help to preserve them for a few more generations.

Make your 'Book of Games of Today and Yesterday' as attractive and stoutly bound as possible. Use illustrations to explain actions as well as for decoration, and make sure everybody contributes. It can go into the school library when it is finished – an incentive for well presented work. If possible, get the notation for the singing games written down; a music specialist should be able to help if this is outside your skill. The children could record their interviewees singing these songs and chants or learn them and pass them on to the class themselves.

## Follow-up
If the book turns out well and you have collected some interesting rhymes, let your local paper know. Publicity could bring you a whole new crop of material, so you could contact the paper early in the project if you would like this kind of feedback.

# Time to vote

**Period**
1900–1918.

**Age range**
Eight to eleven.

**Group size**
Whole class.

## What you need
Copy of *Miss Rivers and Miss Bridges* Geraldine Symons (Macmillan and Puffin) (optional).

## What to do
Choose an issue which is important to the children and suggest that you take a class vote. Then say that you will allow only the boys to vote, but the girls have to abide by the outcome. The ensuing outrage is a good way to begin work on universal suffrage (point out that, at one time, not all men had the vote either).

## Follow-up
Read *Miss Rivers and Miss Bridges* by Geraldine Symons.

# The home front

## Period
1940s.

## Age range
Eight to twelve.

## Group size
Whole class and individuals.

## What you need
Tape, shoe-boxes, card, corrugated card, material, copies of pages 121–122, large sheets of paper, paints, copy of *Carrie's War* by Nina Bawden (Puffin) and *The Evacuees* by B S Johnson (Gollancz) (optional), tape of '40s music (optional).

## What to do
Make your classroom into an exhibition area about the home front during World War II. Children may be able to bring artefacts from home – make sure these are labelled with the child's name and looked after carefully, since many of them will have sentimental value.

Criss-cross the classroom windows with tape, and ask the children why this was done (to protect against flying glass from bomb blasts). In what other ways did people protect themselves? (They built shelters in the garden and put sandbags in front of the window of at least one room.) Make a table-top model of a blitzed street with houses made from shoe-boxes and card in two rows of terraces. Make Anderson shelters from corrugated card for some of the back gardens, and pile sandbags made from scraps of material in front of a window in other houses. Study some photographs of the blitz before deciding where the bomb fell in your model street and what the damage would have been. Then demolish and damage the houses accordingly.

Discuss the messages on propaganda posters: 'Careless talk costs lives', 'Is your journey really necessary?', 'Dig for victory', and so on. Then make some posters for the classroom walls.

Make a ration table showing the weekly rations for a family in your street (see fact box). One of the children may be able to bring in a real ration book but, if not, they are easily made: use buff covers for adults, blue for children and pages of little squares for each commodity.

Why was rationing necessary? Analyse a typical day's meals today to see how much of what we eat is imported. Why was it difficult to import food in the war? What would have happened if goods had not been rationed? Talk about the black market and tell the children how, before the introduction of sweet rationing, there were no sweets to be had in the shops – a few greedy people had them all! But once rationing started, everyone was able to buy a few sweets.

Looking at the ration table, children may wonder whether people had enough to eat. But although food during the war was boring and limited, people always had enough. It is worth contrasting this with the situation in occupied Europe, where people were much worse off.

Clothes were rationed, too. Distribute copies of pages 121–122 and let the children work out the kind of wardrobe that was possible on 48 coupons a year. They could make drawings showing their present wardrobe and a 48-coupon wardrobe.

# Fact box

## Food rationing
Rations varied at different times during the war, but an average weekly ration for each person was:

1s 6d worth of meat
8oz (227g) sugar
4oz (113g) butter, margarine or cooking fat
1 egg
1oz (28g) cheese
2oz (57g) tea

For other items, like tinned food, jam, biscuits, dried fruit, etc, a points system was used. Each person had 20 points a month to spend on these foods which could be bought at any shop. (Basic rations had to be bought at the shop at which you were registered as a customer.) Fish wasn't rationed but was scarce. The sweet ration was 8oz (227g) per month.

## Clothes rationing
Raw materials and labour for making clothes were needed for the war effort so civilian clothes were rationed. The allowance was 48 coupons a year and each item of clothing had a coupon value (see page 121). (Brides got an extra allowance).

Many children had to be evacuated from areas of the country likely to be bombed. Which were these areas? Discuss the choices faced by parents living in danger areas. If they were well off, they could send their children to America or Canada and probably not see them for years, also running the risk of the ship being sunk. Alternatively, they could send the children to safer parts of Britain.

Which option would you have chosen if you had been a parent in World War II? Which would you have preferred if you had been a child during that time?

Try to find someone who was evacuated during the war to come and talk to the class about how it felt. Read *Carrie's War* and extracts from *The Evacuees*.

Get the children to imagine that they are evacuees, and ask them to write about how it feels. What would it be like staying with a strange family? Would they be worrying about their family left behind? What would they miss? What would they take with them to remind them of home? Would it help if they had their brother(s) or sister(s) with them?

You could make a class frieze entitled 'Waiting to be evacuated', with each child contributing a collage or painted figure to the forlorn group. What sort of clothes would they be wearing? What would their luggage look like? There would be no plastic bags or brightly coloured nylon bags, and don't forget the gas masks in cylindrical tins or square cardboard boxes and the labels worn by the children with their names and destinations on them.

Find out what happened in your area durng World War II. Did your town suffer from air raids? What was the extent of the damage? Were there many casualties? The local library should be able to help with this research. Add to your display photocopies of the local paper reporting on any major incidents. Try to find someone who remembers life during the war in your area, to come and talk to the children. Finally, a tape of music from the '40s will add atmosphere to your exhibition.
Note: If anyone brings in a gas mask, do not allow any of the children to try it on – the decaying material in the mouthpiece is dangerous if inhaled.

# Papers past and present

### Period
Twentieth century.

### Age range
Eight to twelve.

### Group size
Five or six.

### What you need
Copies of the local
newspaper (past
and present).

### What to do
Your local library should have a set of local newspapers
going back to the beginning of this century (and often
earlier), either in bound copies or on microfiche. (Getting
copies from microfiche versions may take a week or two,
so allow time for this, and ask for the largest possible
size of copy.)

These newspapers offer a resource which you can use
in many ways for historical work. They are particularly
useful for detailed reports of important local events,
disasters, and so on, from the past, and also for the local
angle on national events.

However, besides using newspapers to look at specific
events, you can use them to make direct comparisons of
everyday life now and in the past.

Get copies of a complete issue of the paper for the
period in which you are interested, and mount and
protect each sheet (so that it can be a permanent
resource for future use, which will justify the expense of
getting the copies made).

Ask the children to compare the pages of the old
newspaper with current copies. You may want to look at
specific topics you have been studying (clothes, food,
houses, etc) or you can let the children pick out the things
they find most interesting. The advertisements are of
particular value – both the displayed and the classified
ads – offering plenty of fascinating information about life
in the past (jobs, prices, fashions, preoccupations).
Children will also find them easier to read than the main
text which, in older newspapers, tends to be too dense for
most young readers.

When you have sorted out how much shillings and old pennies were worth, what a guinea was, and so on, you can ask the children to put what they have found into a wider context, by further research either in reference books or in the paper (Yes, that dress seems very cheap, but have you looked in the job ads to see how much people were earning?) Each child should be able to write a report on 'What I have learned about 19— by reading the (newspaper's name).'

**Follow-up**
Display the reports alongside extra copies of parts of the old newspaper with the items that inspired the report ringed or highlighted.

# Sounds of the century

**Period**
Twentieth century.

**Age range**
Eight to twelve.

**Group size**
Individuals.

**What you need**
Encyclopaedias and reference books.

**What to do**
Write a list of 'trigger words' on the blackboard. Here are some suggestions — you may be able to think of others:

Crystal set

Workers' Playtime

His Master's Voice

Dick Barton, special agent

Alvar Lidell

Children's Hour

Cat's whisker

Lord Haw Haw

Muffin the Mule

This list will probably mean very little to your class. (If you have a knowledgeable child who is bursting to show off his knowledge, persuade him to keep silent for the moment.) Ask the children to choose one or two items on the list and write them down. Now suggest that they ask their grandparents and older friends and relations what the written words mean to them. In this way, most children will find that they have tapped a rich vein of reminiscence about broadcasting and gramophones in the past.

Encourage the children to report back as fully as possible and record the main points on the board. The same trigger will obviously produce similar reminiscences but a more complete picture can be built up from different people's responses to it.

This exercise should be enough to arouse the children's interest in the history of recording and broadcasting.

Now they can set to work with reference books to fill in the gaps. When were gramophones invented? Which came first – gramophones or wirelesses? What sort of wireless programmes were popular? What were gramophone records like? What did an old wireless look like? How did a crystal set work? When was the transistor radio invented? How was it different from the old wireless? When did long-playing records arrive? When did television begin? How old are the people now who had no TV when they were children?

# Fact box

Edison and Bell produced the first gramophone in 1885. It had a huge horn and reproduced sound from a wax-coated cylinder. In 1901 the first flat shellac gramophone record was introduced, and by 1912, the price of these had fallen enough to enable many people to buy them.

In 1903 the tone arm for the gramophone was introduced, and in 1925 the horn disappeared and gramophones were electrified with built-in loudspeakers. Long-playing vinyl discs were developed in 1948 – they had the great advantage of being unbreakable.

Marconi's wireless telegraph had been transmitting morse for several years before the first transmission of human speech by Fessenden in 1902. Marconi developed the wireless and opened the first British public broadcasting station in Chelmsford, Essex, with a concert by Dame Nellie Melba. The BBC's first regular broadcasts started in November 1922. The first *Children's Hour* was heard the following month, and continued until 1964. *Dick Barton* was another children's programme, and was first broadcast in 1946.

'It's being so cheerful . . .' was the catch-phrase of Mona Lott, a lugubrious character in *ITMA*, a comedy show with Tommy Handley, which was broadcast from 1939 until 1949. In its heyday in 1944, 40 per cent of the population listened to it.

Alvar Lidell was one of the most popular BBC wartime announcers, and Lord Haw Haw was the nickname given to the anonymous Englishman (William Joyce) who did propaganda broadcasts for the Germans during the war.

*Workers' Playtime* was a wartime variety broadcast designed for people to listen to while they were at work in factories, etc.

Crystal sets were cheap and simple early wirelesses which people could make for themselves. The cat's whisker was the vital component. You could only listen to a crystal set through headphones, and by about 1925 the swing to valve sets had begun.

Baird's first television transmission was in 1926. In 1930 the BBC broadcast the first fully synchronised TV programme. In 1935 the old 30-line broadcasts ceased, and in 1936 new systems were broadcast from Alexandra Palace.

By the time of King George VI's coronation in 1937, there were about 10,000 viewers. Television broadcasts ceased on 1 September 1939 (because the transmitter was a perfect direction-finder for the enemy during the war), and the service was not resumed until 1946. At this time there were ten million radio licence holders, but only a few thousand TV licence holders.

*For the Children*, the first TV programme for children was broadcast in July 1946, and the popular *Muffin the Mule* the following October.

It was during the fifties that television really expanded. The first colour TV broadcast was seen in America in 1929, but colour TV sets did not really become widespread until about 1970. The first regular colour broadcasts began on BBC 2 in 1967.

# History from family photos

## Period
Twentieth century.

## Age range
Six to twelve.

## Group size
Individuals or pairs.

## What you need
Copies of family photographs,
copies of page 123
for children to take home,
clear plastic envelopes
or heavy-duty plastic
to make these,
sticky tape,
small numbered sticky labels.

## What to do
Send a letter (see page 123) to parents asking them or any other relatives to lend family photographs for use in a class history project.

When the photographs come in, check that they are clearly named; if not, name them yourself immediately. Put each picture in a plastic envelope with a piece of card to keep it flat, and cover any details written on the back. Number the envelopes and list the photographs brought by each child with their numbers and details copied from the backs of the pictures. Seal the envelopes firmly with sticky tape and keep them in a safe place when not in use. You can make simple envelopes from heavy-duty plastic covering — the kind that is used to protect sweaters, mattresses, and so on, in shops.

The way you use these pictures depends very much, of course, on what you get. You could make a worksheet referring to a suitable selection of pictures, which might include questions and instructions like these:

**1** Write a list of the ways in which the clothes in pictures 1, 2 and 5 are different from clothes worn by children today.
**2** Which do you think is the older picture — number 4 or number 8? Why?
**3** Can you put pictures 3, 5, 9, 10, 17 and 20 in order of date? Write down the numbers in order with the oldest first.
**4** There is something in picture 14 that shows it was taken during World War II. What is it?
**5** Write down three ways in which the car in picture 11 is different from cars today.
**6** You know the street that is shown in picture 16. Make a list of the shops which are still there and another list of the shops which have disappeared. About when do you think this picture was taken?
**7** The child in picture 20 is a boy. Would you have guessed that? How old do you think he is? Do boy babies ever wear dresses today? If so, when? This picture was taken in 1902. Can you find out when boys of this age stopped wearing dresses.
**8** When do you think picture 19 was taken? How would you describe the hairstyles of the people in the picture?

## Follow-up
When the children have completed their investigations, ask them to pick out the pictures they found most interesting and prepare a quiz. Pool ideas for quiz questions, duplicate quiz sheets, display the pictures attractively, and then invite other classes and parents to come along and try your quiz.

# Reproducible material

# Clues for history hounds, see page 10

## Norman

Look for . . .

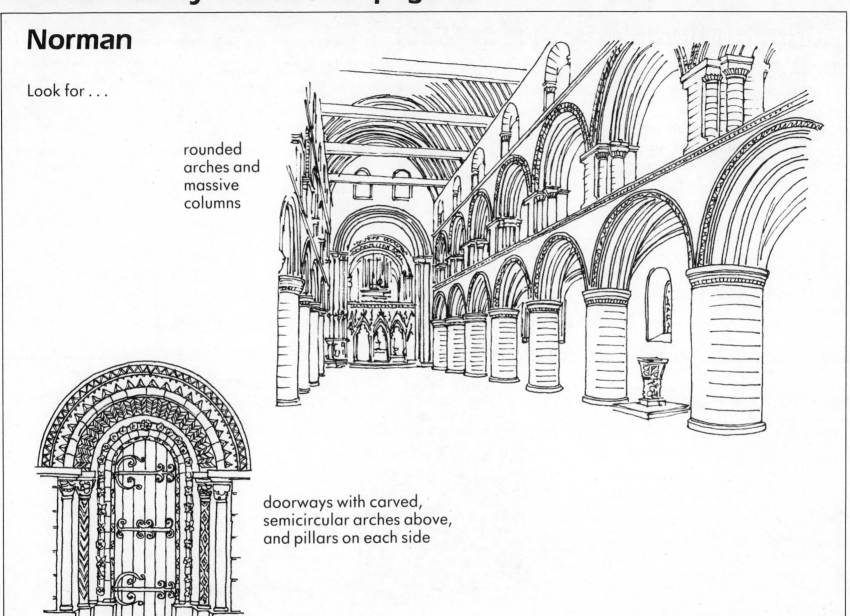

rounded
arches and
massive
columns

doorways with carved,
semicircular arches above,
and pillars on each side

## Gothic (Middle Ages: 1150–1550)

In houses of this period, the roofs were made of timber, not stone. Look for wooden beams and half-timbering.

Early Gothic churches are simple (Early English). Later the stonework is more complex and windows are larger (Decorated). At the end of the period you find panelled decoration, flying buttresses and fan vaulting (Perpendicular). Look for . . .

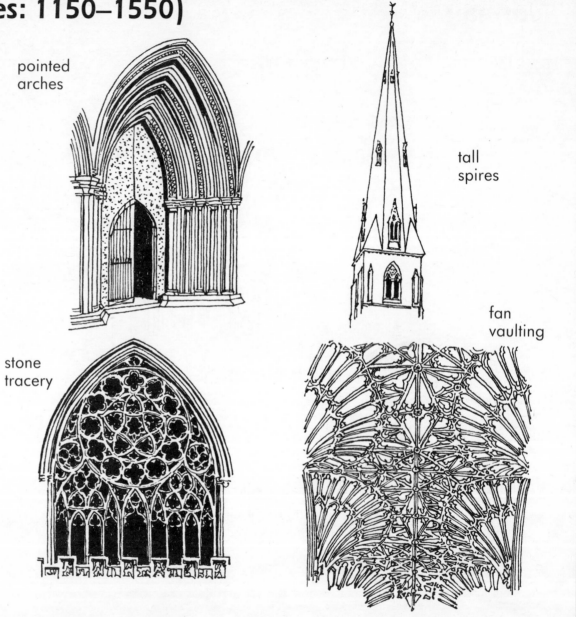

pointed arches

tall spires

fan vaulting

stone tracery

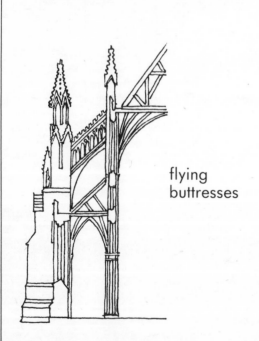

flying buttresses

## Elizabethan and Jacobean (1550–1625)

This was the time when many of the great country
houses were built. Look for half-timbering again,
and . . .

ceilings with elaborate plaster panels

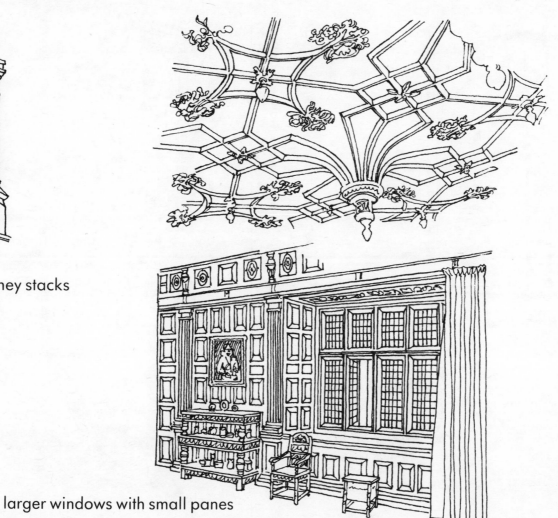

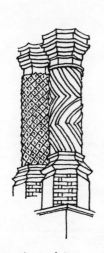

decorative chimney stacks

larger windows with small panes

# Turning the spit, see page 24

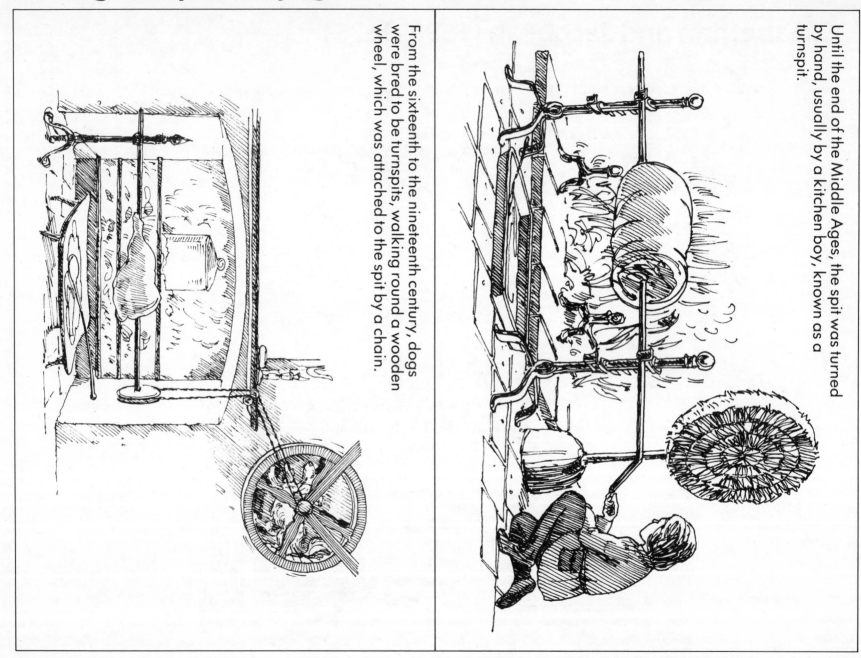

Until the end of the Middle Ages, the spit was turned by hand, usually by a kitchen boy, known as a turnspit.

From the sixteenth to the nineteenth century, dogs were bred to be turnspits, walking round a wooden wheel, which was attached to the spit by a chain.

# Roman numerals, see page 27

## Roman numerals

Since about 1500 we have used Arabic numerals to write down our numbers, but before that Roman numerals were used. You may see them on old milestones and gravestones, in old books and on many clocks and watches.

Roman numerals are made up from letters:

| | |
|---|---|
| I = 1 | C = 100 |
| V = 5 | D = 500 |
| X = 10 | M = 1,000 |
| L = 50 | |

You may know the Roman numerals from 1 to 12 from clocks:

I   II   III   IV (or sometimes IIII)   V   VI   VII   VIII   IX   X   XI   XII

As you can see, it is very important to notice in which order the letters are shown:

|     | IX = 9 (one before ten) |
|-----|-------------------------|
| but | XI = 11 (one after ten) |
| so  | XL = 40 (ten before fifty) |
| but | LX = 60 (ten after fifty) |

Here are some more Roman numerals with their Arabic equivalents:

| | |
|---|---|
| XVIII = 18 | CC = 200 |
| XXXII = 32 | DCLXX = 670 |
| LIV = 54 | MCMLIX = 1959 |
| LXXI = 71 | MCMLXXXVII = 1987 |
| LXXXIX = 89 | |

Can you work out what the following numbers are? Try it with a friend. The answers are upside down at the bottom of the page.

XXI   XLII   XCI   LXX   CIX   CCCXXIII   MDC   MCMXXI

You could make up a Roman numeral quiz for your friend.

Answers: 21   42   91   70   109   333   1600   1921

# Egyptian number chart, see page 32

| 1 | 2 | 3 | 4 | 5 | 6 | 7 | 8 | 9 | 10 |
|---|---|---|---|---|---|---|---|---|---|
| I | II | III | IIII | IIIII | IIIIII | IIIIIII | IIIIIIII | IIIIIIIII | ∩ |

| 11 | 15 | 22 | 39 | 100 | 1000 | 10,000 |
|---|---|---|---|---|---|---|
| I∩ | IIIII∩ | IIII∩∩ | IIIIIIIII∩∩∩ | 𓏤 | 𓆼 | 𓂭 |

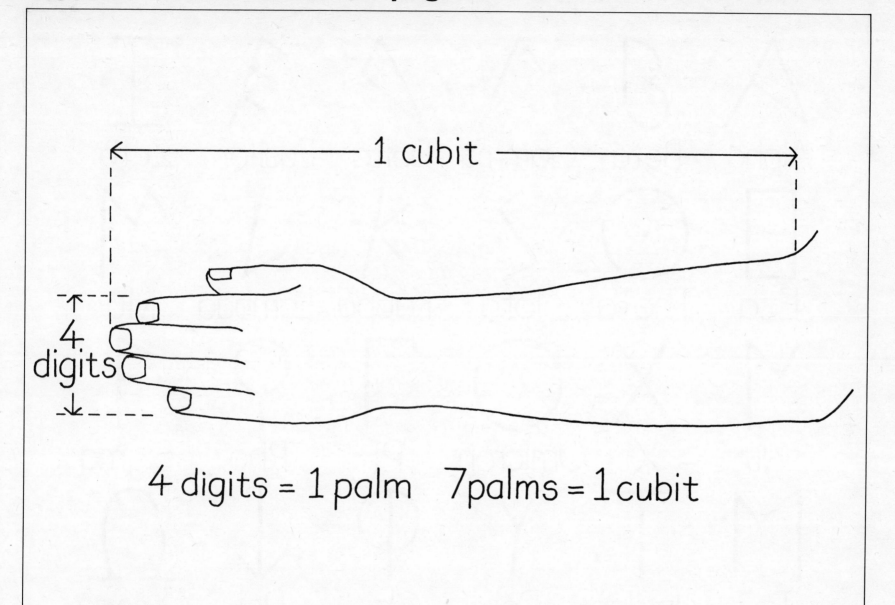

1 cubit

4 digits

4 digits = 1 palm   7palms = 1 cubit

# Greek alphabet, see page 33

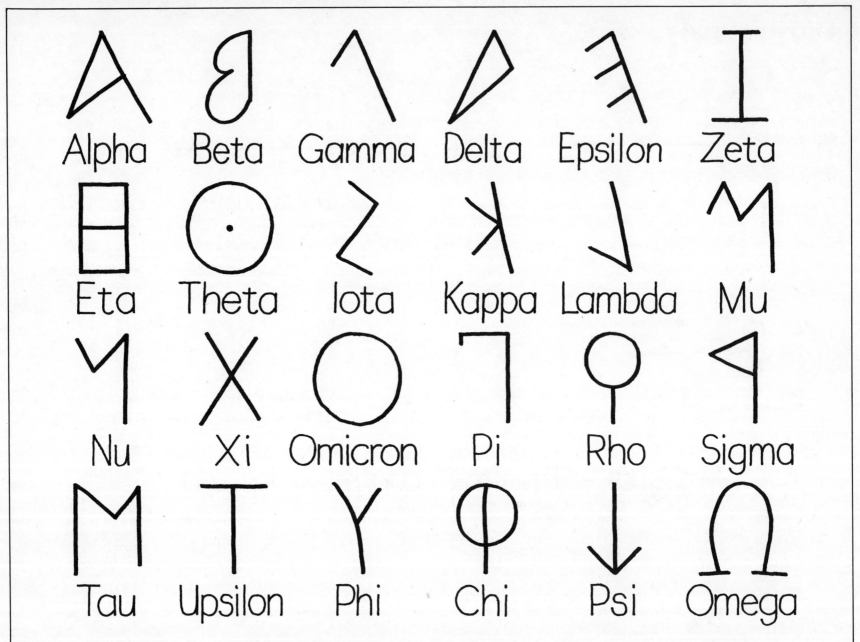

Alpha   Beta   Gamma   Delta   Epsilon   Zeta

Eta   Theta   Iota   Kappa   Lambda   Mu

Nu   Xi   Omicron   Pi   Rho   Sigma

Tau   Upsilon   Phi   Chi   Psi   Omega

## Old mile quiz

**Different miles that were used in the Middle Ages:**

English mile = 6,610 yards (10 furlongs)
London mile = 5,000 yards
Irish mile = 2,240 yards

Welsh mile = about four modern miles
Scottish mile = 1,976 yards

Use this list and a calculator to help you answer the quiz below.

*There was a crooked man and he went a crooked mile,*
*He found a crooked sixpence against a crooked stile.*

**1** How far did the crooked man go (in yards) if he was using an old English mile?

**2** Roger Bannister was the first man to run the mile in four minutes. If he had managed the same speed for an old Welsh mile, how long would it have taken him?

*How many miles to Babylon?*
*Three score and ten.*
*Can I get there by candlelight?*
*Yes, and back again!*

**3a** How many miles is it to Babylon in old Irish miles?
  **b** If I go there and back, how far will I go in Roman miles (to the nearest mile)?

**4** The longest river in Scotland is the Tay at 117 miles. How long would the Scots in medieval times have said it was (to the nearest mile)?

*Five miles meandering with a mazy motion*
*Through wood and dale the sacred river ran.* Coleridge

**5** If Coleridge had been measuring in old English miles, how far would his sacred river have run in modern miles (to the nearest mile)?

A modern nautical mile is nearly 2027 yards

Roman mile = 1618 yards

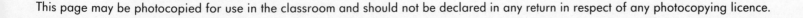

# Norse runes, see page 48

a b d e f g h i k l m n o p r s t thu y

Inscription on a stone slab at Maughold, Isle of Man.

Inscription on a tombstone found at St Paul's London.

Inscription on a comb case found in Lincoln.

Inscription on a sword hilt found at Greenmount, Ireland.

## Old Norse-English word list

a – owns
auk – and
eftir – in memory of
fina – Finna (a name)
hethin – Hedin (a name)
kamb kothan – a good
  comb

kiari – made by
krus thino – this cross
lekia – down
let – put
lifilt – Lifilt (a name)
selshofoth – Seal'shead
  (a name)
seti – set up
soer theta – this sword
stin thensi – this stone
thorfastr – Thorfast
  (a name)
tomnal – Dufnall (a name)
tuki – Tuki (a name)
tutor sino – his daughter

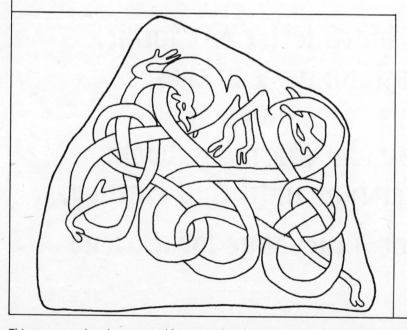

𝕬 𝕭 𝕮 𝕯 𝕰 𝕱 𝕲 𝕳 𝕴 𝕵 𝕶 𝕷 𝕸
𝕹 𝕺 𝕻 𝕼 𝕽 𝕾 𝕿 𝖀 𝖁 𝖂 𝖃 𝖄 𝖅

𝖆 𝖇 𝖈 𝖉 𝖊 𝖋 𝖌 𝖍 𝖎 𝖏 𝖐 𝖑 𝖒 𝖓 𝖔 𝖕 𝖖 𝖗 𝖘 𝖙
𝖚 𝖛 𝖜 𝖝 𝖞 𝖟

1 2 3 4 5 6 7 8 9

This kind of writing is called black letter or Gothic. The first books printed in England were in this kind of type. By 1700, printers were using type more like the type we use today. In Germany books were still printed in black letter type until this century.

Can you write your name or a message for a friend in this kind of writing?

# Illuminated manuscript, see page 59

In the days before printing was invented, all books had to be copied by hand. This was usually done by monks. Sometimes they decorated the pages with beautifully coloured illustrations. They liked to take a capital letter, make it extra large and draw little pictures inside it and around it.

Here are some copies of fourteenth century illuminated manuscripts.

# Coat of arms, see page 60

Only certain colours and patterns can be used in heraldry. These are listed below. When you are choosing the colours for your coat of arms, remember these rules: you must not put a colour on a colour or a metal on a metal or a fur on a fur.

This coat of arms was made up by a pupil. She chose black (*sable*) for the background (*field*) of her shield, and has put a gold (*or*) chevron on it. She has shown three loaves of bread in white (*argent*) for her name (Susan Baker), and three trefoils in green (*vert*) because she is a keen Guide. The official description (*blazon*) of her coat of arms might be: sable, on a chevron or between three loaves argent, three trefoils vert.

## Metals
Or – gold or yellow
Argent – silver or white

## Furs
Vair – white on blue
Ermine – black on white

## Colours
Gules – red
Azure – blue
Sable – black
Vert – green
Purpure – purple

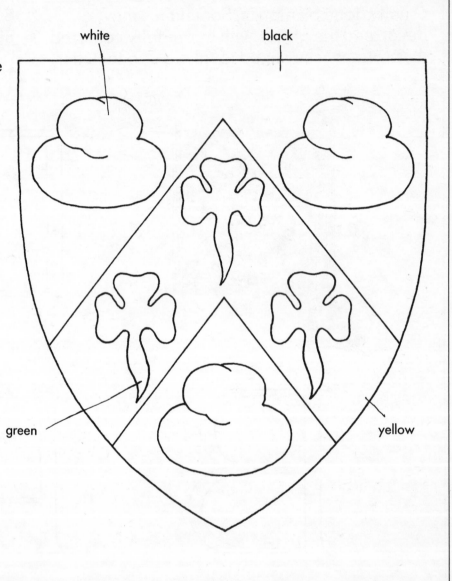

# Coat of arms, see page 60

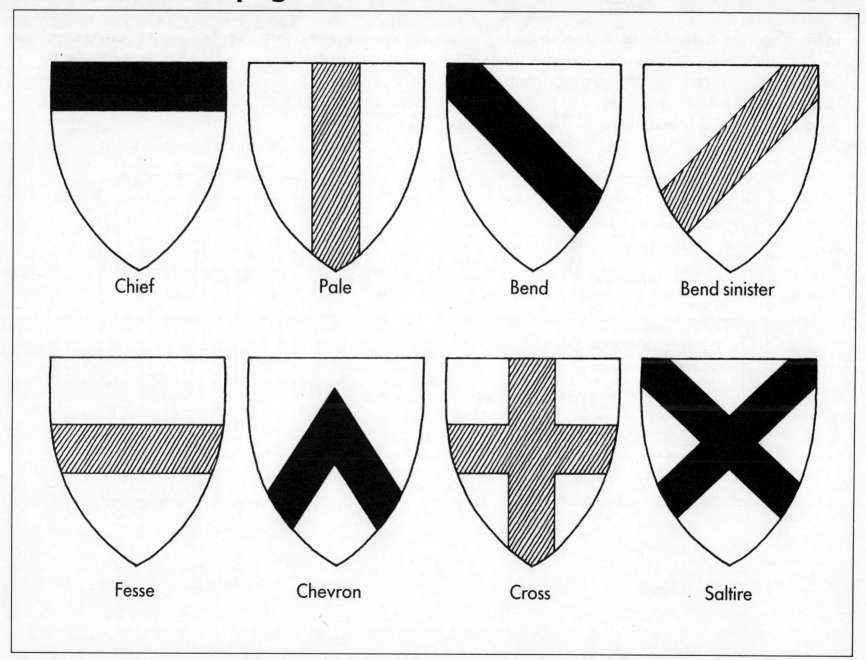

Chief

Pale

Bend

Bend sinister

Fesse

Chevron

Cross

Saltire

# Horn book, see page 63

In the fifteenth, sixteenth, seventeenth and eighteenth centuries when books were rare and expensive, children learned to read from horn books. These had a single sheet of paper fixed to a paddle-shaped piece of wood. The paper was covered with a thin sheet of horn (from a cow's horn) to protect it.

Here is a picture of a horn book. Can you make one like it?

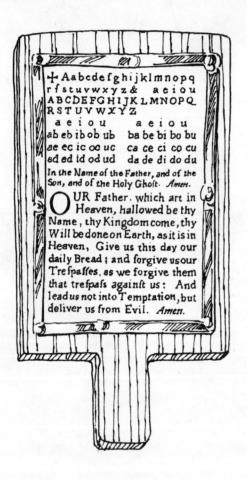

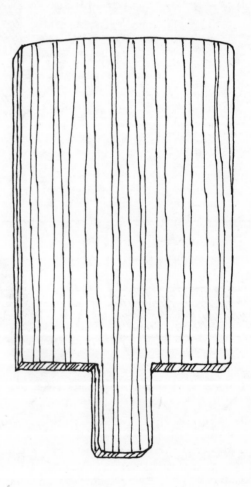

The vij day of Octobar, beynge Satowrdaye, anno 1564, at viij a cloke at nyghte, was sene comynge out of ye northe easte very great lyghtes lyke great flames of fyre, whiche shott forthe as it (were) gonepowdar fyeryd and spred out in a longe frome ye northe easte, northe, and northe west, in dyvars placis at once; and all mett in ye mydes of ye fyrmament, as it war ryght ovar London, and desendyd somewhat west warde, and all ye flames beynge ther gatheryd grew in to a rednys, as it were a very sangwyn or blode cowlar, and this contynewyd tyll ix of ye cloke; and all ye same nyght was more lyghtar then yf ye mowne had shone moste bryght, wheras no mone shone that nyght, for yt chaungyd but one day before, whiche was Fridaye.

Anno Domini 1564, Master Newalle, Deane of Powles, preachyd at Polles Chrose ye 19 of Novembar, where he protestyd that ther was not one trew worde in Master Dormars boke latly browght ovar from beyonde ye seas.

The 20 of Novembar, beynge Monday, in ye mornynge, a bowt vj of ye clocke, throughe neglygence of a mayden with a candell, ye snoffe ther of fawlynge into an hundryd wayght of gonne pothar, thre howssys in Bucklersbury war sore shaken, and ye backar partes of ye same howsys wer all to blewne and shattard in pecis, and ye afore sayde mayde was so byrnt that she dyede ther of with in ij dayes afftar; yf this powthar had bene in a sellar, as it was in a garret, it had donne myche more harme.

In the yeare of our Lord 1562, ye 8 day of Septembar, was a pryste taken (by sertayn promotars and my Lorde of Elies men) for sayienge of masse in Fettar lane at my Lady Cares housse, whiche pryste was violently taken and led (as ten tymes wors than a traytur) thwrowe Holburne, Newgate markyt, and Chepsyd to the Cowntar at the stokes callyd the Pultrie, with his masse boke and his porttoys borne before hym, and ye chalice with the paxe and all othar thyngs, as myche as myght make rewde poople to wondar apon hym. And the nomber of people was exsedynge great that folowyd hym, mokynge, derydynge, cursynge, and wyshynge evyll to hym, as some to have hym set on ye pelory, some to have hym hangyd, som hangyd and qwarteryd, some to have hym byrnt, sum to have hym torne in pesys and all his favorars, with as myche violence as the devill collde invent, and myche more then I can wryte, but well was he or she that cowld get a plucke at hym or gyve hym a thumpe with theyr fyst or spyt in his face.

## Putting the Union Jack together

white    red

The cross of St George (England)

blue    white

The cross of St Andrew (Scotland)

white    red    blue    white

First Union flag 1606

white    red    gold

Commonwealth flag 1649

white    red

The cross of St Patrick (Ireland)

Union Jack 1801

# Union Jack, see page 69

Colour in these three flags and then cut them out along the dotted lines. Can you fit them on top of each other to make the Union Jack? Which two will you use to make the first Union flag?

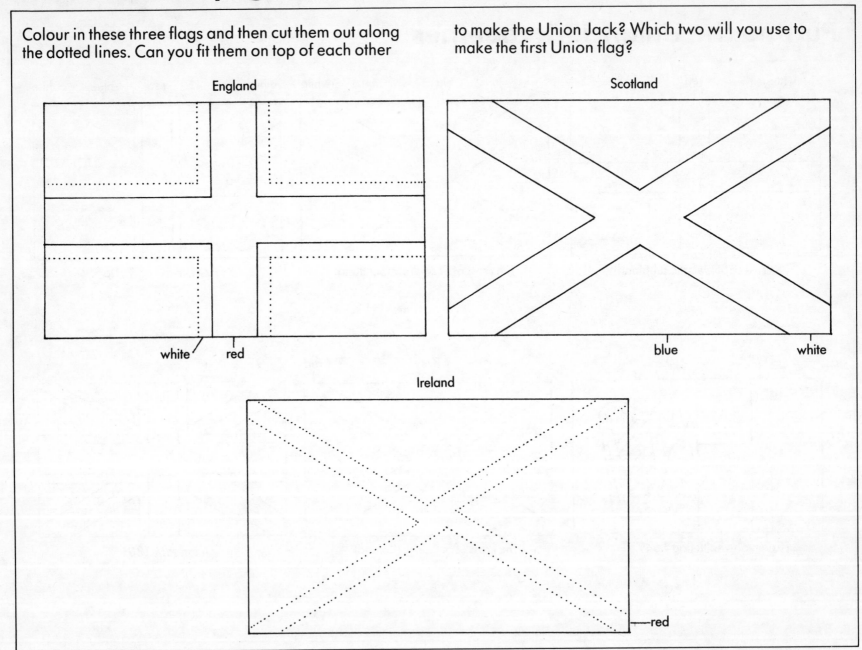

England

white    red

Scotland

blue    white

Ireland

red

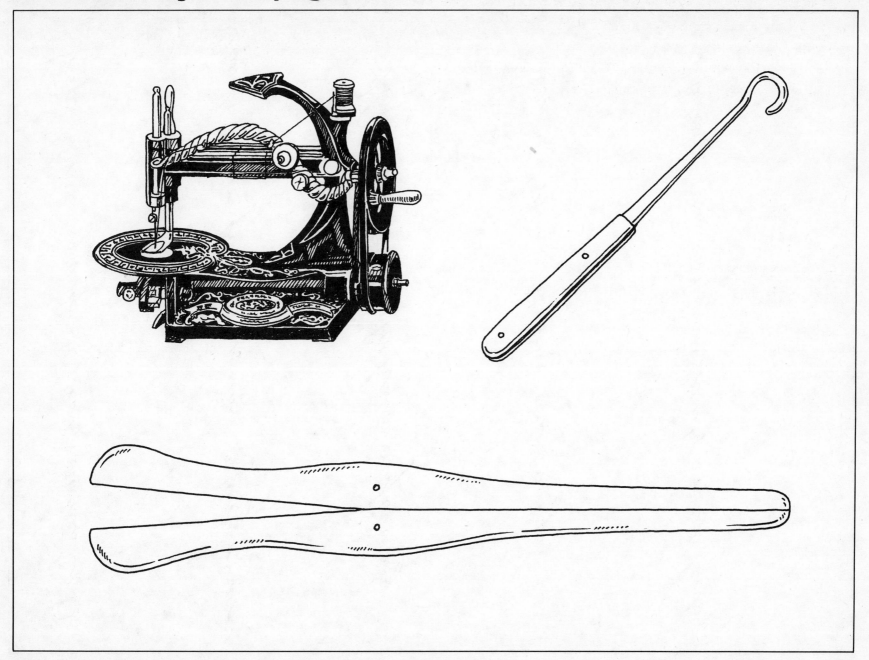

Impatience aggravates misfortunes C D,

One bad companion ruins many men

Never short with pain or poverty

Quarrelsome persons are dangerous

Modesty ornaments beauty and talents

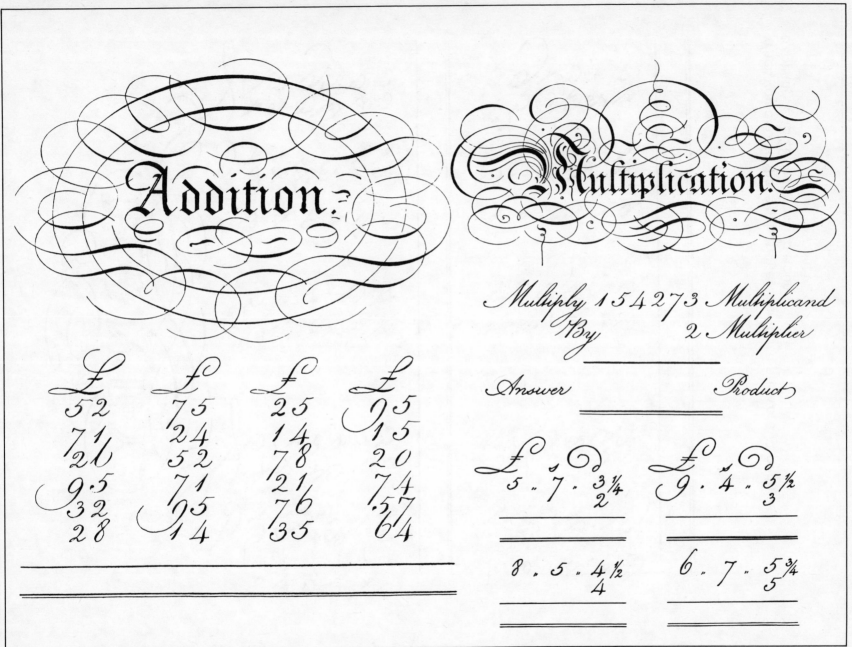

*Addition.*

*Multiplication.*

Multiply 154273 Multiplicand
By        2 Multiplier

Answer            Product

| £ | £ | £ | £ |
|---|---|---|---|
| 52 | 75 | 25 | 95 |
| 71 | 24 | 14 | 15 |
| 21 | 52 | 78 | 20 |
| 95 | 71 | 21 | 74 |
| 32 | 95 | 76 | 57 |
| 28 | 14 | 35 | 64 |

| £ | s | D |
|---|---|---|
| 5 . 7 . 3¼ | | 2 |

| £ | s | D |
|---|---|---|
| 9 . 4 . 5½ | | 3 |

| £ | s | D |
|---|---|---|
| 8 . 5 . 4½ | | 4 |

| £ | s | D |
|---|---|---|
| 6 . 7 . 5¾ | | 5 |

**MONEY.**

| £ | s | d |
|---|---|---|
| 71 | 14 | 6 |
| 52 | 17 | 7 |
| 93 | 15 | 8 |
| 96 | 12 | 7 |
| 34 | 13 | 11 |
| 35 | 12 | 9 |

| £ | s | d |
|---|---|---|
| 5 | 3 | 3½ |
| 3 | 4 | 4½ |
| 4 | 7 | 4½ |
| 7 | 2 | 3¾ |
| 4 | 3 | 3½ |

| £ | s | d |
|---|---|---|
| 34 | 15 | 8 |
| 72 | 17 | 4 |
| 96 | 14 | 3 |
| 46 | 12 | 10 |
| 34 | 13 | 7 |
| 58 | 19 | 6 |

| £ | s | d |
|---|---|---|
| 52 | 16 | 8 |
| 95 | 14 | 6 |
| 13 | 13 | 4 |
| 56 | 19 | 2 |
| 12 | 4 | 3 |
| 54 | 14 | 9 |

| £ | s | d |
|---|---|---|
| 4 | 7¼ |  |
| 3 | 3¾ |  |
| 9 | 2 |  |
| 10 | ⅓ |  |
| 7 | 2 |  |
| 9 | ½ |  |

| £ | s | d |
|---|---|---|
| 43 | 12 | 5 |
| 74 | 15 | 6 |
| 35 | 14 | 9 |
| 24 | 16 | 7 |
| 95 | 17 | 8 |
| 25 | 19 | 9 |

When you add up these lists, remember that there were 12 pennies in a shilling, and 20 shillings in a pound.

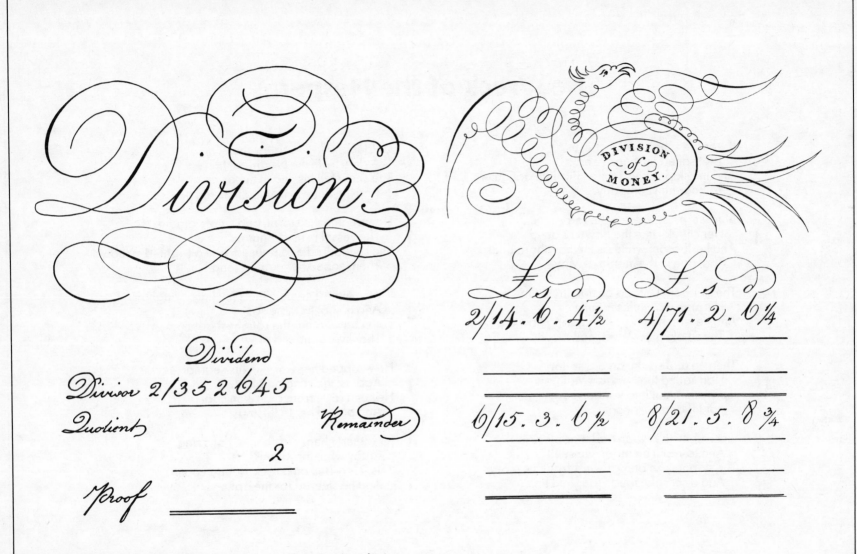

*Division*

DIVISION of MONEY.

Dividend
Divisor 2/3 5 2 6 4 5        Remainder

Quotient

2

Proof

£ s d          £ s d
2/14 . 6 . 4½      4/71 . 2 . 6¼

6/15 . 3 . 6½      8/21 . 5 . 8¾

To obtain the proof, multiply the quotient by the divisor
and add on the remainder.

# The Wreck of the Hesperus

1
It was the schooner Hesperus,
    That sailed the wintry sea;
And the skipper had taken his little daughter,
    To bear him company.

4
Blue were her eyes as the fairy-flax,
    Her cheeks like the dawn of day,
And her bosom white as the hawthorn buds
    That ope in the month of May.

3
The skipper he stood beside the helm,
    His pipe was in his mouth,
And he watched how the veering flaw did blow
    The smoke now West, now South.

1
2
Then up and spake an old sailor,
    Had sailed the Spanish Main,
'I pray thee put into yonder port,
    For I fear a hurricane.

2
1
'Last night, the moon had a golden ring,
    And to-night no moon we see!'
The skipper, he blew a whiff from his pipe,
    And a scornful laugh laughed he.

1
Colder and louder blew the wind,
    A gale from the North-east;
The snow fell hissing in the brine,
    And the billows frothed like yeast.

1
Down came the storm, and smote amain
    The vessel in its strength;
She shuddered and paused, like a frighted steed,
    Then leaped her cable's length.

3
'Come hither! come hither! my little daughter,
    And do not tremble so;
For I can weather the roughest gale
    That ever wind did blow.'

1
He wrapped her warm in his seaman's coat
    Against the stinging blast;
He cut a rope from a broken spar,
    And bound her to the mast.

4
3
1
'O father! I hear the church-bells ring,
    O say what may it be?'
''Tis a fog-bell on a rock-bound coast!'
    And he steered for the open sea.

**4** 'O father! I hear the sound of guns,
   O say what may it be?'
**3** 'Some ship in distress, that cannot live
   In such an angry sea!'

**4** 'O father! I see a gleaming light,
   O say what may it be?'
**1** But the father answered never a word,
   A frozen corpse was he.

**1** Lashed to the helm, all stiff and stark,
   With his face turned to the skies,
The lantern gleamed through the gleaming snow
   On his fixed and glassy eyes.

**4** Then the maiden clasped her hands and prayed
   That savèd she might be;
And she thought of Christ, who stilled the wave
   On the Lake of Galilee.

**1** And fast through the midnight dark and drear,
   Through the whistling sleet and snow,
Like a sheeted ghost, the vessel swept
   Towards the reef of Norman's Woe.

**1** And ever the fitful gusts between
   A sound came from the land;
It was the sound of the trampling surf,
   On the rocks and the hard sea-sand.

**1** The breakers were right beneath her bows,
   She drifted a dreary wreck,
And a whooping billow swept the crew
   Like icicles from her deck.

**1** She struck where the white and fleecy waves
   Looked soft as carded wool,
But the cruel rocks, they gored her side
   Like the horns of an angry bull.

**1** Her rattling shrouds, all sheathed in ice,
   With the masts went by the board;
Like a vessel of glass, she stove and sank,
   Ho! ho! the breakers roared!

**All** At daybreak, on the bleak sea-beach,
   A fisherman stood aghast,
To see the form of a maiden fair,
   Lashed close to a drifting mast.

**All** The salt sea was frozen on her breast,
   The salt tears in her eyes;
And he saw her hair, like the brown sea-weed,
   On the billows fall and rise,

**All** Such was the wreck of the Hesperus,
   In the midnight and the snow!
Christ save us all from a death like this,
   On the reef of Norman's Woe!

## The Village Blacksmith

Under a spreading chestnut tree
  The village smithy stands;
The smith, a mighty man is he,
  With large and sinewy hands;
And the muscles of his brawny arms
  Are strong as iron bands.

His hair is crisp, and black, and long,
  His face is like the tan;
His brow is wet with honest sweat,
  He earns whate'er he can,
And looks the whole world in the face,
  For he owes not any man.

Week in, week out, from morn till night,
  You can hear his bellows blow;
You can hear him swing his heavy sledge,
  With measured beat and slow,
Like a sexton ringing the village bell,
  When the evening sun is low.

And children coming home from school
  Look in at the open door:
They love to see the flaming forge,
  And hear the bellows roar,
And catch the burning sparks that fly
  Like chaff from a threshing floor.

He goes on Sunday to the church,
  And sits among his boys;
He hears the parson pray and preach,
  He hears his daughter's voice,
Singing in the village choir,
  And makes his heart rejoice.

It sounds to him like her mother's voice,
  Singing in Paradise!
He needs must think of her once more,
  How in the grave she lies;
And with his hard, rough hand he wipes
  A tear out of his eyes.

Toiling,—rejoicing,—sorrowing,
  Onward through life he goes;
Each morning sees some task begin,
  Each evening sees it close;
Something attempted, something done,
  Has earned a night's repose.

Thanks, thanks to thee, my worthy friend,
  For the lesson thou hast taught!
Thus at the flaming forge of life
  Our fortunes must be wrought;
Thus on its sounding anvil shaped
  Each burning deed and thought!

# What was it like when you were young?, see page 79

1 What sorts of things did you learn at school?

2 What were your teachers like?

3 How did you get to school?

4 What time did you get up and go to bed?

5 What toys did you have and what games did you play?

6 Can you remember any playground rhymes or songs?

7 What sort of things did you have to eat?

8 Did you have any jobs to do at home?

9 What happened on your birthday/at Christmas/during holidays/on Sundays?

10 What was the best treat you ever had?

11 Did you have pocket money?

12 If so, what did you spend it on?

13 What did you wear in summer/in winter?

14 What happened when you were naughty?

15 When did you start work?

16 What was your job?

17 Where did you live when you were my age?

18 Which year were you born?

19 What are the biggest changes you have seen in your life?

20

21

22

23

24

25

# Clothes rationing, see page 82

## Clothes rationing in World War II

During the war it wasn't only food that was rationed. Clothes were rationed too.

Wool, cotton and other materials were all needed for the 'war effort', and workers in the clothing factories had to make uniforms for the forces. So civilians could only have a very limited number of clothes.

Each person had 48 clothing coupons a year, and each item of clothing had a coupon value. So when people went shopping they had to decide whether they really could afford to spend their precious coupons on the piece of clothing they wanted.

At the bottom of the page there is a list of the coupon values of various clothes during the war.

Make a list of all the clothes you have, and work out how many coupons they would be worth. You will probably find that it is far more than 48.

### Coupon values

| | |
|---|---|
| Shoes and football boots 2 | Dress 5 |
| Socks 1 | Trousers 6 |
| Pants 2 | Sweater 5 |
| Pyjamas 6 | Blazer or jacket 6 |
| Shirt or blouse 4 | (8 if lined) |
| Gym tunic 4 | Raincoat 7 (10 if lined) |

# Clothes rationing, see page 82

Now make a list of a new set of clothes for yourself that would only take 48 coupons. You could make a drawing showing your present wardrobe and your ration wardrobe.

Perhaps you can understand why there was so much 'make do and mend' during the war. Clothes were handed on from one person to another. They were unpicked and made up as something else. Sweaters were unravelled and the wool reknitted. Everything was patched, darned and mended over and over again. Nothing was wasted.

# Letter to parents, see page 89

Dear

The children are doing a twentieth century history project and we should be most grateful if you could lend us any photographs you have that were taken between 1900 and about 1960.

We should particularly like to have photographs showing:
local scenes,
fashions which were very extreme,
children in different types of clothes,
children playing,
interiors of houses,
people at work,
street scenes,
anything that looks very different from today's equivalent or anything that may give the children an insight into the past — or make them laugh!

Wedding groups are least useful because styles in wedding clothes tend to change more slowly than styles of other clothes.

Please make sure that all the pictures have your name on them and, if possible, a date or approximate date. We should be delighted, of course, if you could add a short written note about any of the pictures explaining any points of interest.

We will look after all the pictures very carefully; they will be sealed in plastic envelopes before the children are allowed to look at them.

When we have studied the pictures, we hope to hold a small exhibition with a quiz devised by the children based on the historical points they have noticed, to which parents will be invited. If you do not want your pictures included in the exhibition, perhaps you would write 'not for exhibition' on them.

We hope that the children will learn a lot from this project and we shall be most grateful for any help you can give.

Yours sincerely

# Resources

The Usborne Book of World History ed A Millard (Usborne 1985).
History of Britain series P Sauvain (Macmillan 1982) Books 1–4.
Archaeology J Cooke (Wayland 1983).
Times of the Pharaohs P Vernus (Hart Davis 1980).
Great Civilisations – Ancient Greece C Fagg (Longman 1978).
Enjoying Archives D Iredale (Phillimore 1985).
The Invaders J West (Ward Lock 1986).
The Romans ed H Pluckrose (Hamish Hamilton 1981).
The Vikings ed H Pluckrose (Hamish Hamilton 1981).
Heraldry T Rowland-Entwhistle (Granada 1984).
The Superbook of Flags G Beal (Kingfisher 1986).
Medieval Times ed M Lodge (Hodder & Stoughton 1981).
The Bayeux Tapestry N Denny and J Filmer-Sankey (Collins Educational 1966).
Homes in History M Harrison (Wayland 1983).
Home Sweet Home E Allen (A & C Black 1979).
Here's the Church P Watkins and E Hughes (Julia Macrae 1980 op).
Toppers History series (Macdonald 1977 op) The Story of Books V Driscoll.
The Food We Eat J Cochrane (Macdonald 1975).

Shopping in History S Robertson (Wayland 1984).
Just Look at Clothes B Ralph Lewis (Macdonald 1986).
At School and in the Country in 1900 S Purkis and E Merson (Longman 1981).
An Edwardian Household S Ross (Wayland 1986).
Machines in History A Nahum (Wayland 1985).
The Encyclopaedia of Inventions ed D Clarke (Marshall Cavendish 1977 op).
Family Life from 1930 to the 1980s F Wilkins (Batsford 1985).
How We Used to Live 1935–53 F Kelsall (Macdonald 1981).
Children in the War E Merson, S Echlin and S Purkis (Longman 1983).
Britain Since 1945 C Gardiner (Oliver & Boyd 1985).
Supersubs History J Graham and B Musselwhite (Jonquil 1986).
The Shell Book of Firsts Patrick Robertson (Michael Joseph 1983).
Bright Ideas Resource Handbook (Scholastic Publications 1987).

op Out of print, try libraries.

# Acknowledgements

The editors and publishers extend grateful thanks for the reuse of material first published in Art & Craft and Junior Education to: Robin Capon for 'Roman plaques'; G Roland Smith for 'Toga time'; Leon Metcalfe for 'Bayeux bas relief'; Robert Crozier for 'Egg-box knights'; Ian Smith for 'Writing the runes'; Jane Lawrence for 'Modern mummies', 'Egyptian mathematics', 'Egyptian measurement' and 'Popular myths'; Andrew Bryden for 'Horn books', 'Elizabethan houses', 'Quill pens' and 'Motte and bailey castle model'; Michael Pollard for 'Change of clothes'; John Davis and Warren Farnworth for 'Shop signs'; Eric Simpson for 'Signposts to the Vikings'; Beatrice Myers for 'Going Greek 1–6'; Graeme Kent for 'Recreating the past'; Brian Moses for 'The home front'; John West for 'Picturing the past'; Morag Henriksen for 'Reporting on the Romans'.

Every effort has been made to trace and acknowledge contributors. If any right has been omitted, the publishers offer their apologies and will rectify this in subsequent editions following notification.

# Indexes

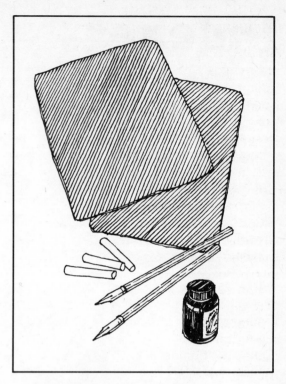

# Topic index

# Other Bright Ideas titles

Previous titles in this series available are:

Bright Ideas Seasonal Activities
0 590 70831 7          £5.45

Bright Ideas Language Development
0 590 70834 1          £5.45

Bright Ideas Science
0 590 70833 3          £5.45

Bright Ideas Christmas Art and Craft
0 590 70832 5          £5.45

Bright Ideas Reading Activities
0 590 70535 0          £5.45

Bright Ideas Maths Activities
0 590 70534 2          £5.45

More Bright Ideas Christmas Art and Craft
0 590 70601 2          £5.45

Bright Ideas Classroom Management
0 590 70602 0          £5.45

Bright Ideas Games for PE
0 590 70690 X          £5.45

Bright Ideas Crafty Moneymakers
0 590 70689 6          £5.45

Bright Ideas Music
0 590 70700 0          £5.45

Bright Ideas Assemblies
0 590 70693 4          £5.45

Bright Ideas Writing
0 590 70701 9          £5.45

Bright Ideas Lifesavers
0 590 70694 2          £5.45

Bright Ideas Christmas Activities
0 590 70803 1          £5.45

Bright Ideas Spelling
0 590 70802 3          £5.45

Set of any six titles          £27

Write to Scholastic Publications Ltd,
Westfield Road, Southam, Leamington Spa,
Warwickshire CV33 0JH, enclosing your
remittance. Make cheques payable to
Scholastic Publications Ltd.